blue
rider
press

THE REPUBLIC
of CONSCIENCE

THE REPUBLIC
of CONSCIENCE

GARY HART

BLUE RIDER PRESS

an imprint of Penguin Random House

New York

blue
rider
press

An imprint of Penguin Random House LLC
375 Hudson Street
New York, New York 10014

Copyright © 2015 by Gary Hart
Penguin supports copyright. Copyright fuels creativity, encourages diverse voices, promotes
free speech, and creates a vibrant culture. Thank you for buying an authorized edition
of this book and for complying with copyright laws by not reproducing, scanning,
or distributing any part of it in any form without permission. You are supporting
writers and allowing Penguin to continue to publish books for every reader.

The author gratefully acknowledges permission to reprint an excerpt from
"From the Republic of Conscience" in *Opened Ground: Selected Poems 1966–1996*
by Seamus Heaney. Copyright © 1998 by Seamus Heaney. Reprinted
by permission of Farrar, Straus and Giroux, LLC.

Blue Rider Press is a registered trademark and its colophon
is a trademark of Penguin Random House LLC

ISBN 978-0-399-17523-7

Printed in the United States of America
1 3 5 7 9 10 8 6 4 2

BOOK DESIGN BY NICOLE LAROCHE

While the author has made every effort to provide accurate telephone numbers,
Internet addresses, and other contact information at the time of publication, neither
the publisher nor the author assumes any responsibility for errors, or for changes that
occur after publication. Further, the publisher does not have any control over and does
not assume any responsibility for author or third-party websites or their content.

For a generation of United States senators
who put the interests of the American Republic first

No porters. No interpreter. No taxi.
You carried your own burden and very soon
your symptoms of creeping privilege disappeared.

. . .

At their inauguration, public leaders
must swear to uphold unwritten law and weep
to atone for their presumption to hold office—

—SEAMUS HEANEY,
"From the Republic of Conscience"

CONTENTS

IIIIIIIIIIIIIIIIIIIIIIIIIIIIIIIIIIIIIIIIIIIIIIIIIIIIIIIIIIIIIIIIIIIIIIIIIII

THE CORRUPTION OF THE AMERICAN REPUBLIC AND THE RENEWAL OF FIRST PRINCIPLES

America's founders created a republic knowing that it, like all republics from ancient Athens and Rome onward, would be vulnerable to corruption. From 400 BC onward, corruption of the republican ideal took the form of narrow, individual, and special interests taking precedence over the common good and the commonwealth. Our founders knew that if this evil insinuated itself into the new American Republic, our nation would not long survive in the form they had designed and had hoped for it.

By these classic standards, the American Republic in the twenty-first century is massively corrupt. A vast and cancerous network of lobbying, campaign fund-raising, and access to policy makers in administrations and lawmakers in Congress is based purely and simply on special and narrow interests. This tragedy is compounded by two relatively recent trends: More than four hundred former members of Congress, not to mention their spouses and family members, have joined the lobbying ranks; and former administration officials come and go from one administration to another with periods of lobbying activities in between.

Thus, a permanent political class has established itself in our nation's capital. Whether incestuous is an appropriate description or not, it is most certainly a system that an increasing number of Americans distrust—and with considerable reason. Friends promote friends. Rolodexes are shared. Networks are maintained. The system is increasingly closed to outsiders, or at least to outsiders who have yet to attain membership. National leadership appears to be limited to a few families.

Such a permanent political system rarely produces innovative policies or creative agendas. To contest for a seat in the United States Senate, even in a medium-size state such as Colorado, requires millions, sometimes tens of millions, of dollars. Very little of that sum is produced by small contributions. Most of it comes from the institutional investors and political action committees with specific agendas that have proliferated in both political parties. Senators and members of Congress spend hours each day telephoning large contributors, pleading for money. Television networks routinely decry this trend even though they are the principal beneficiaries of the hundreds of millions of dollars spent on political advertising.

To raise these staggering sums requires a candidate to subscribe to established agendas. Those agendas do not represent the national interest. They represent a panoply of special interests. Successful candidates arrive in office heavily beholden to those interests that have contributed. Their flexibility, creativity, and imagination are circumscribed by whatever commitments had to be made to finance a campaign. At the very least, they have traded access, the coin of the political realm, for campaign contributions.

But this is not the kind of government our founders created and envisioned for future generations. Even a casual reading of the Constitutional debates, speeches, and voluminous correspondence reveals the founders' deep concerns, based on their intimate familiarity with the theorists of the republic from Athens through Machiavelli to the English and Scottish Enlightenment, over the threat of corruption, the danger to all republics.

We can only imagine what Washington, Adams, Hamilton, Madison, and Jefferson, among many others, would say about today's American Republic. Being pragmatists, they would recognize that a nation that increased a hundredfold in population in two centuries, that adapted itself to world leadership after World War II, and that now struggles to compete in a globalized economy would have to change and adjust. But they also knew the difference between policy that must adapt to new realities and principles that must not.

Indeed, they believed that the first principles of every constitution must be frequently renewed to prevent corruption. And the necessity for a timely renewal of principles is the central purpose of this book.

As a veteran of campaigning, holding public office, and advising various administrations, I find no justification in our Constitution for the political system we have now created or have permitted to be created by others. Instead, this system is the product of the refusal to enact campaign finance reforms, to restrict transition from public office to lobbying, and to provide limited candidate access to free media. This is not a mysterious or complex secret process everyday Americans cannot understand. It is the product of interest groups who prefer to trade cash for access, television networks who prefer paid political advertising to open access to the public airwaves, hugely lucrative lobbying organizations, and the compounding of this corrupt system by recent Supreme Court decisions.

Out of this entire morass, nothing would dumbfound a returning founder more than decisions by the current Supreme Court allowing corporations to contribute unlimited amounts of money to promote their particular narrow interests. This stands as nothing more nor less than the highest judicial body in the Republic sanctioning the corruption of that Republic.

This book attempts to contrast the Republic our founders created and hoped would be perpetuated with the government we now have. Each area of legislation and policy today is dominated by the interest groups concerned with it. Rather than starting with a view of what is best for the nation long-term, the common good, legislators and policy makers seek to reconcile the demands of each narrow interest concerned with that issue. Being men of experience, our founders anticipated this, but they wanted those governing our nation to consider the demands of particular interests in the broader context of the national interest. They feared the corruption that inevitably results when governance becomes nothing more than a process for satisfying an endless host of particular interests. This accounts for their insistence on "disinterested" representatives.

The disappearance of a sense of the national interest, and the consequent governance by and for special interests, reflects itself in today's political process through the channeling of hundreds of millions of dollars from interest groups to lobbyists and then to officeholders and office seekers. The result is the rise of a permanent political class increasingly remote from everyday Americans and a system that could lead to the ultimate destruction of the republican ideal. This is the corruption we were warned about from our earliest beginnings that would destroy the American Republic.

The new realities of the twenty-first century do not require the United States to abandon the principles upon which it was founded. Neither our economic foundation, nor our foreign policy, nor our national defense requires a corrupt political system. Indeed, commitment to the commonwealth and the common good, including a growing economy, an enlightened foreign policy, and strong national security, will make us more successful and will attract the favorable opinion of mankind.

Preservation and renewal of those first principles represent the duty we owe our founders to keep the Republic they bequeathed to us and our posterity.

THE REPUBLIC
of CONSCIENCE

INTRODUCTION

This is a book about a republic—the American Republic—
what it was meant to be and what it has become. In some
crucial respects the twenty-first-century American Republic is
not the country our founders thought they had created.

The search for the causes of the increasing gap between
word and deed starts with an understanding of what a republic actually is or ought to be.

At their best, republics, including ours, have demonstrated
four basic qualities: popular sovereignty; a sense of the common good; demonstration of civic virtue by its citizens; and
resistance to the forces of corruption.

Popular sovereignty, of course, means that all political
power ultimately rests with the people. A sense of the commonwealth involves an appreciation for all those assets and
resources held by all the people—public properties and the
public institutions that preserve them. Civic virtue means per-

formance of the duties of citizenship to maintain the integrity of the republic and protect the rights it provides. And corruption historically meant placing narrow, special, or personal interests ahead of the common good in government.

By gauging the twenty-first-century American Republic against these standards, ones universally accepted by our founders, we can begin to understand where and how America today is falling short and why so many Americans feel something is missing, that something has gone wrong.

If America is not living up to its promise, it is important to know how and why.

The corruption feared by our founders is insidious. Once members of Congress lose sight of the common good and enter the never-ending realm of narrow interests and ensuring their own reelections, that narrow, self-interested view becomes apparent to all in government and permeates the administrative bureaucracy. As a leading *New York Times* columnist wrote in the fall of 2014: "Getting elected and raising money to get re-elected—instead of governing and compromising in the national interest—seems to be all that too many of our national politicians are interested in anymore." He attributes laxness in the Secret Service and lackadaisical performance throughout government to the lack of performance and purpose among elected officials: "It actually looks as if they came to Washington to get elected so they could raise more money to get re-elected. That is, until they don't get re-elected. Then, like the former House majority leader, Eric Cantor, they can raise even more money by cashing in their time on Capitol Hill for a job and a multimillion-dollar payday from a Wall Street investment bank they used to regulate."

That is the current state of American politics in a nutshell. And it is not what America's founders had in mind for this nation. The ancient fear of the corruption of the republic was caused by the knowledge that when self-interest replaced the common good and the national interest, a republic would no longer survive. And this is why it matters.

It would be illusory to believe that a large majority of Americans spend much time comparing our founding beliefs and ideals with our performance in the twenty-first century. But few would dispute that we are experiencing a moment in our history, like few others before, when we seem unmoored and adrift.

There are certainly economic discomforts and failures, dismal political performances, and constricting options in managing world affairs today. It will require the passage of time to be able to look back and properly analyze and describe the American experience during our current time. The purpose of this book is to explore the possibility that our disquiet is caused by a deep sense that we are becoming, or perhaps have become, a different kind of nation than we believe ourselves to be.

If this is so, even to a degree, then it is worth asking *how* and *why*. The thoughts offered here in response to these questions are a reflection of one American's long life combining public service and private endeavor, learning and teaching in the academy, and, most of all, writing and thinking.

I can personally testify that American politics have taken a distinctly downward turn in the space of one mature lifetime. Many in my generation entered public service directly as a result of President John F. Kennedy's challenge to give part of our lives in service to our country. Whether he realized it or not, and I believe he did, this challenge had its roots in the republican ideal from ancient Athens. Republics rise or fall depending on the exercise of responsibility and duty by their citizens. We have not heard that challenge for more than half a century.

My reflections are those of a political fundamentalist, not an "originalist" of the judicial kind but a citizen who cannot help but take the ideas of those who founded this country seriously. I believe the founders meant what they said and wrote, and I believe they identified the character of our nation with the precepts, principles, systems, and ideals they laid down as our foundation. To depart measurably from them is to become a different nation.

My belief that our founders were pragmatists has been confirmed over and over again by scholars much more learned than I. Being pragmatists, the founders knew that change is the essence of human existence. Very little stays the same, and certainly almost nothing abides in the chaotic evolution, revolution, and upheaval in the human struggle to structure governments.

So the founders would be the first to advise that we adapt our systems and our policies to the realities of the current age. Though libraries could be filled with lists of the differences between the early twenty-first century and the late eighteenth, policies and programs, at home and abroad, must still flow from a system of value—in our case, values built upon notions of equality, fairness, duty, rights, and the common good that do not change.

Thus, it matters whether we have sacrificed those values to expediency, the corner cutting brought on by urgency, immediacy, shortsightedness, and impatience. New realities require new economic ideas, new defense structures, new technologies, new ways of dealing with other nations. But new realities do not require a nation founded on ancient ideals of the republic to become a different kind of nation. We call people who remake themselves for the moment chameleons. Like individuals, nations can sacrifice their core identity out of false information, rigid ideology, expediency, a desire to demonstrate power, and even greed. This is why serious consideration of our present-day performance against the backdrop of our historic values is a necessary undertaking.

There is an additional argument for reviewing our present condition. The founders intended that the republic they were creating have a life beyond them. They drafted and adopted a Constitution whose very preamble makes it clear they were establishing a nation "to ourselves *and our posterity*." To a crucial degree, the republic they bequeathed to future generations can perpetuate itself only by the adherence of their posterity to the principles and ideals built into its governing documents, structures, and institutions.

Even as we pay tribute to the system of government bequeathed to us by our founders, we acknowledge that the nation they created was far from perfect. Slavery, foremost, but also equal rights for women, voting rights, and many other shortcomings had to be confronted—often in conflict—and overcome. But our nation's successful struggles to resolve these shortcomings are reasons for encouragement.

Much of our nation's nobility has to do with the relationship of the citizen to his or her government and the opportunities for practical participation in government our founding system provides. Despite civil wars and bitter social and political struggles, all conducted before a global public, Americans can be proud of hard-won progress in achieving our claims for ourselves.

First: access. The enfranchisement of women a century ago, the Voting Rights Act of 1965, and lowering the voting age to eighteen have dramatically opened the doors to full participation in American democracy. For several decades, states have made access to the polls much easier. Unfortunately, we are in yet another period of retrenchment when, for blatantly political motives, laws are being enacted to make voting more difficult. Despite protestations that these exclusionary laws and practices are to prevent voter fraud, of which there is virtually none, the clear purpose of those leading the retrenchment is to disenfranchise minorities, those living on the margin, and those with less education.

Second: transparency. In the last quarter of the twentieth century, citizen groups struggled to open closed political doors. Legislative sessions became more open. Cable television provided wide coverage of activities of the House and Senate. Latter-day muckrakers disclosed questionable practices and shady dealings. Public disclosure of destructive business practices led to a generation of sweeping environmental laws, safeguards against corrupt practices, worker health-and-safety regulations, increased regulation of financial markets (until these were subverted in the 1990s), and greater accountability on the part of policy makers, legislators, and administrators. This is a never-ceasing struggle. The forces of self-interest always prefer the corridors of power to be dark.

Third: military transformation. Nothing is so hard as to

change traditional and conservative institutions. Our military is no different. The services and their supporters rightly argue that they have kept our nation secure—that is, until Vietnam and 9/11. Vietnam was never a threat to our security and we encountered a form of warfare there that was unfamiliar to us. 9/11 continued this revelation by proving our nation vulnerable to terrorists using unconventional means of attack.

A few reformers began to call for changes in military thinking as early as the mid-1970s. Few would listen. Then-junior officers with experience in Vietnam rose in the ranks and began to achieve senior commands and the long, slow process of transformation began. It has been accelerated by the experiences of another generation of junior officers who have served in Iraq and Afghanistan. As a result, we now have a de facto fifth military service built around special forces. It is called the Special Operations Command and it links SEALs, Delta Force, Army Rangers, and the Air Force's special forces.

Special Operations now forms the tip of the security spear and will increasingly be tasked with responding to low-intensity, unconventional conflicts carried out by stateless nations using cities as their battlefields. This military transformation is historic and will prove its worth in coming days. It does not necessarily improve our standard of living, but it does better protect it.

Finally: though much of this book focuses on the corrupting influence of large-scale corporate donors and special interest money in politics, there is a faint glimmer of hope even in a dark tunnel. The most positive innovation in recent American political practice is the raising of small contributions largely through the Internet. This breakthrough first occurred on a notable scale in the first Barack Obama presidential campaign in 2008 and returned in even larger form in his reelection effort in 2012. There are also Internet websites springing up—ActBlue, for example—that specialize in raising small-donor funds and channeling them to Democratic candidates. Over ten years, ActBlue has raised and distributed more than $600 million. Even this innovation, however, has a dubious side; some of its funds go into the so-called Super PACs that have come to dominate American politics.

Even though there have been some areas of genuine progress, objectivity requires us to carefully examine the areas where our deeds and our performance fall far short of our promise and our principles, and where the spotlight of world public opinion reveals the largest gaps in our national conduct. This is the beginning of the hard road. Honesty about our shortcomings is as important as an equally candid assay of our achievements, what genuinely we can be proud of.

Only after placing failures and successes on the national scales can we see the road ahead and decide whether we will choose to continue on the hard road of continued struggle to form a more perfect union or be content with the smooth road of just getting along.

Not only is our government now almost totally focused on the thousands of particular industries, companies, interest groups and their narrow agendas, an iron-clad, copper-riveted link has also been forged connecting attention to those agendas with the staggering sums of money contributed by those interest groups to election campaigns for president, the Senate, and the House of Representatives. Much like efficient plumbing, American politics is becoming a closed system. And the realization of how destructive that closed system is has led to the rise of Tea Partiers and Occupiers alike.

Everyday citizens, even those who pay dues to one or more of the national groups that hire expensive lobbyists, shake their heads with wonder and disgust at the conspicuousness of the system's corruption and the equation of successful manipulation of the laws with staggeringly expensive and unrewarding political campaigns. How airtight this system has become and how closed to sunlight's disinfectant is measured by the hundreds of former members of Congress and the thousands of their staff now enriching themselves at the lobbyists' trough.

It is a national shame and it is, to employ a much misused term, a scandal.

The founders' ideal of the *disinterested* legislator and executive will never be reestablished until this closed political plumbing system is totally replaced. Until then, our national spirit will be strangled by this legalized corruption. And their reference to "disinterested" does not mean *uninterested*. They meant having no personal interest in a policy or legislative outcome. Today, there is too little distance between a legislator's votes and his or her complex personal and financial interests, including future employment in the vast lobbying empire.

And, despite the progress in governmental transparency, recent political maneuvering, especially the Supreme Court's *Citizens United v. Federal Election Commission* decision, is now cloaking money in politics under new clouds of secrecy. Our systems of government, including proceedings in the House and Senate and in their committees, may be more open and visible, but how those elected to the Congress finance their campaigns is now more opaque, mysterious, and easily manipulated.

Until we have the courage to punish the corrupt and rid ourselves of a system that entwines interest groups, the lobbying octopus, and campaign coffers, we will continue to fall far short of our national expectations and promise, and our government will be corrupt and corrupted.

Social justice is in decline. Even though the ancient republic accepted social classes and our own Republic took seventy-five years from its founding to begin to lift the yoke of slavery, our ideal has always been, especially since the Great Depression, that a safety net of some proportion should not let the elderly, the young, and the incapacitated fall by the wayside. Since reaching a plateau in our economic performance in the 1970s, however, we have entered a cynical cycle most bluntly known as "devil take the hindmost." When our economy is not growing, those least able to look after themselves are the first thrown overboard under the banner of slogans such as "A thousand points of light" or "We must balance our budget" or "We can't afford handouts" or "We must eliminate waste, fraud, and abuse." Never mind that these are all rhetorical devices to facilitate an escape from harsh reality with our conscience intact.

Those not afraid to look disturbing facts head-on know that one in five American children, or more than 16 million children, are in poverty, that 15 percent of the national population or 46.5 million Americans are in poverty, and that the plight of the elderly is deepening. These statistics are now so well known that they numb our minds. But even numbed minds find it difficult to reconcile the spectacular wealth at the top with both the poverty that plagues a quarter of the American population and the belief that we have the most fair and just society on earth.

At stake is the notion of progress and whether government has a role in bringing it about. He who controls the meaning of words defines the debate. George Orwell, among others, understood this very well. "All animals are equal. Some are more equal than others," for example. When partisan media chatterers demonized the very legitimate word "liberal," most Democrats substituted the word "progressive" to describe their policies and beliefs. Therefore, it is worth exploring the meaning of "progress" and "progressive."

One of my earliest memories is of humble men appearing at our back door toward the end of the Great Depression politely asking for a bite of food. We lived near the railroad tracks that ran through Ottawa, Kansas, and when trains stopped, these knights of the road, gaunt as any figures from *The Grapes of Wrath*, would go to back doors nearby, always back doors, and ask for any help—ask, not beg—that we might give. My mom would give them a slice of bread, usually with a little sugar on it, and butter if we had it. Their remembered gratitude brings sadness these many decades later.

This was brought to mind by a recent *New York Times* story about how even the most ardent critics of government spending still depend on it. Spending for the poor has gone down even as spending for the middle class, including those in the Tea Party, has gone up. "They are frustrated that they need help, feel guilty for taking it, and resent the government for providing it," the story says. That sentence sums up early twenty-first-century American politics better than any other explanation available.

One honest conservative man said: "It's hard to beat up on the government when they've been so good to you. I've never really thought about it, I guess." Could we do without the social safety net, without Social Security and Medicare, without farm subsidies, without unemployment compensation, without school lunch programs, without housing assistance? Of course we could. But we would not be a civilized society and we would not be an American nation any of us would be proud of.

We have freedom of speech. But that speech is most persuasive when it is honest and not hypocritical. Any argument a Tea Party member wants to make is worth listening to, so long as that person is not rich and so long as that man or woman has given up reliance on the government programs that virtually all of us depend on. The anger in America today has much to do with those who depend on the government, who feel guilty for it, and who resent the government for making them feel guilty.

The simple answer is: Get over it. Years ago I had a slogan: "If you want the government off your back, get your hands out of its pockets." People in this country can't have it both ways. Either we do away with the safety net that almost every American depends on or we pay for it. If there is a third option (other than the long-discredited "We must eliminate waste, fraud, and abuse"), let's see it.

In a famous Commonwealth Club speech in his first presidential campaign in 1932, Franklin Roosevelt captured the ambivalence of business toward government: "For while it has been American doctrine that the government must not go into business in competition with private enterprises, still it has been traditional, particularly in Republican administrations, for business urgently to ask the government to put at private disposal all kinds of government assistance. The same man who tells you that he does not want to see the government interfere in business—and he means it and has plenty of good reasons for saying so—is the first to go to Washington and ask the government for a prohibitory tariff on his product."

Recent polls show that many voters who supported Tea Party candidates in 2010 now consider it a mistake because they didn't expect them to be total obstructionists. They are in that large group represented by the man who said: "I never really thought about it, I guess." It's probably too much to ask that those middle-class complainers be as grateful for the support our government, and our taxpayers, provides them as those poor but decent and honest men at our back door were those many years ago.

Ralph Waldo Emerson said that every society has a party of memory and a party of hope. Progress, according to the *Oxford English Dictionary*, is: forward movement, advance, development, improvement; and progressive is: moving forward, proceeding step by step, rapid reform, modern, efficient. Not too bad a description of Emerson's party of hope.

Much of American history can be traced through efforts to move forward, to progress, while preserving the best of our past. Abandon historical institutions, beliefs, and social norms and you become rootless. Hold on to the past and refuse to adapt, and you fail to innovate and create a better society. This seems so commonsensical that it causes you to wonder what the bitter political clashes of today are all about.

They are about government. Conservatives want government to protect them and otherwise leave them alone. In such a laissez-faire, every-man-for-himself nation, a few will rise and the rest are on their own. The rest, of course, includes the elderly, children, and the disabled. Since this philosophy has no room for a social contract, private charity ("A thousand points of light") picks up the pieces. As is often pointed out, this philosophy leaves no room for food inspection, health-and-safety protections, clean-water laws, bank-deposit insurance, and a host of other public services the vast majority of citizens favor.

When asked about the impact of her severe reductions in government service on society, Margaret Thatcher said: "There is no such thing as society." She bypassed Orwell altogether and cut to the quick. If there is no society, there is no need for government. Hobbes is calling the shots: Nature is red in tooth and claw; life is war of all against all; man is wolf to man; and devil take the hindmost. There is little room for progress in the predator nation.

For those of us idealistic enough to believe in such a thing as society and that society can progress, public institutions that form our government are required. Bill and Debbie Shore, founders of a private charity called Share Our Strength, have fed hundreds of thousands, probably millions, of children at home and abroad. But they would be the first to say that our government must bear the major burden of guaranteeing a civilized society and that private charity must do all it can to fill in the gaps when the nation abandons concern and responsibility.

For those who believe that, in a society, that to some degree or other we are all in this together, there are three choices: resist change and retreat to the past; stagnate; or progress. So far, no one has discovered how to progress without the institution of government. Democratic societies exhibit qualities of justice, equity or fairness, mutual respect, concern for the dependent, civility, and the bonds of humanity. Thatcher was correct: If you wish to rid yourself of government, first rid yourself of the idea of society.

Since the 1970s, working- and middle-class family incomes have stagnated as wealth has steadily migrated upward into fewer and fewer hands. This migration continued even during the post-2008 recession. This is not a sustainable path toward the goals of opportunity, justice, and equality. Concentrated wealth is being directed into financial engineering, offshore banks, international investment and production, tax avoidance, and gilded yachts. It is not being invested in America's workers, infrastructure, or next-generation production.

"Widespread poverty and concentrated wealth cannot long

endure side by side in a democracy," wrote Thomas Jefferson. Producing great wealth is one thing. Seeing to its just allocation is quite another.

Corruption of the American Republic radically shifts political power to special interests, but even more perilously it concentrates wealth in the hands of the few.

Early twenty-first-century American discontent results from a deep sense of fundamental unfairness. An unfair society is an unjust society. Systemic unfairness and injustice are incompatible with a stable republic.

For the past three decades our political system, under both political parties, has operated for the benefit of concentrated economic power—banks, investment funds, and a range of financial institutions. As a result of deregulation of the financial sector—a direct result of lobbying, including by former members of Congress and their staffs, and extensive campaign contributions—hundreds of billions of dollars migrated to the top of the financial pyramid.

Everyday Americans paid the price in unemployment, housing foreclosures, and lost pensions. There is no greater illustration of unfairness produced by political corruption.

And it is the central reason why a large segment of the American people are discontented with their government, a government that systematically embraces a corrupt culture that destroys republics such as ours.

Loyal Americans have every right to be angry, and many of us are.

Throughout our history Americans have been skeptical of government, skepticism interspersed with cynicism. We are skeptical when we suspect the worst behind closed doors. We are cynical, as we are today, when our political system transparently and unjustly rewards wealthy and powerful elites and undermines the principles upon which our nation is founded.

We cannot hope to achieve the purpose of our nation the way our government is working today. There is a fundamental incompatibility between government by self-interest, greed, and closed networks on the one hand and a living, functioning republic of engaged citizens preserving the commonwealth on the other. Corruption, seeking to satisfy narrow interests, destroys every sense of community, common good, and nationhood. Ancient political philosophers and America's founders understood that a republican form of government could not survive corruption by special interests.

A republic, including the original American Republic, is an ideal, one that can never be achieved absolutely but one that must always be made "more perfect." There will always be a struggle between self-interest and the common good. In present day America, self-interest is controlling our government and the ideal of the republic is languishing in disrepair and, for its few advocates, in despair. Few political leaders today can be found proclaiming the ideal of the true republic against the overwhelming forces of greed, special interests, and corruption.

Perhaps this is so because idealism itself is misunderstood in an era dominated by acquisition and consumption. An ideal is intangible. It is found only in the mind and the heart of those who keep its flame alive. Anyone who teaches the notion that America itself, governed as an uncorrupted republic, is our purpose must contend with social values of individualism, materialism, and self-actualization. Politics today is almost totally an occupation devoted to wealth and power.

Americans identify with one another most closely under threat, the threat of economic collapse as during the Great Depression or the external threat of military attack. Otherwise we choose to go our own way and not be bothered by common concerns or by problems of governance. Into the vacuum of being left alone, the forces of wealth and power, of special interest and narrow purpose, have entered. And those forces now control the government of the United States.

Are we a society or not? If we are, a social contract is required among civilized people that prevents members of that society from being abandoned by the wayside. Between 1932 and 1974, a majority of Americans believed we were a society with social obligations. Since then, a majority of Americans have questioned that belief and have received considerable encouragement from partisan and ideological media to believe instead that our government cannot and should not create a just society.

A widespread belief in many parts of the world that America teeters on the brink of lawlessness is encouraged by the high levels of random violence in our country. The attempt to deal with a sizable drug culture and its criminal syndicates of suppliers using incarceration as the centerpiece of a "war on drugs" has only managed to warehouse a phenomenal number of minor offenders in national and state prisons. Although efforts are under way to reduce sentences, there are still no serious alternatives to street-corner drug dealing as a way of life for too many unemployed young men.

Rates of recidivism remain high and economic opportunities remain low. Mass incarceration has failed as a social policy, yet alternatives have yet to be found. The widely promoted belief that our economic and justice systems are the best will continue to be undercut by both the drug culture and the rampant reliance on private weapons arsenals as the answer to personal security.

We join such advanced nations as China, North Korea, Iran, and Saudi Arabia in practicing capital punishment, the death penalty, though there is no demonstrable evidence that it deters crime. This is very sad company for the enlightened democracy we claim to be. We live in the hope that a majority of Americans will wake up to the fact that creating jobs is less expensive than building and operating prisons.

Since the dawn of the Cold War in the late 1940s, and the establishment of the national security state during that same period, America has been on a semi-war footing, first against the Soviet Union and then against amorphous and dispersed islands of terrorism. In both pursuits, our nation has violated the civil liberties of its citizens and conducted a bewildering array of covert operations, up to and including torture, in the name of national security.

Arguably, nothing in the history of the United States has caused world opinion to question our values more than these activities. The history of abuses ranges from J. Edgar Hoover's FBI spying on and harassing antiwar and civil rights organizations to "dirty tricks" in the Nixon years to a wide range of covert operations by the CIA to a bewildering Iran-Contra scheme in the Reagan years to waterboarding and torture in pursuit of the "war on terrorism" to massive collection of personal communications data by the National Security Agency.

All this and much more has been justified, once revealed, by various administrations of both political parties as necessary to protect our country. But security has become an expedient excuse for the violation of Constitutional guarantees. Both political parties share blame for placing the easy road of expediency over the hard road of principle.

A s a more or less mature nation, we should have learned by now to think beyond the short-term appeal of trendy political ideas. Take, for example, "supply side" tax cuts. The product of a single line written on a cocktail napkin roughly three decades ago, the promise was that tax cuts stimulated investments, investments created jobs, and employed people would pay income taxes sufficient to cover the budget short-falls of the original cuts.

For those who didn't care for government very much, including Ronald Reagan and George W. Bush, the concealed agenda was to "starve the beast," namely to create deficits that would require shrinking if not eliminating New Deal and Great Society safety nets. Remember "privatization" of Social Security?

So, we cut taxes under both those administrations. And then, under the second Bush, we went to war—twice. Wars cost money. To hide their costs at a time of expanding deficits brought on by the tax cuts, the wars were fought "off bud-get." Let's not incorporate war costs into the budget because that will make the deficit look *really* big.

Then two new developments piled on: the housing bubble and bank speculations, and the Tea Party. Suddenly, even the assurances of a Keynesian convert such as Richard Cheney ("deficits don't matter") weren't good enough. Deficits were evil even during a recession, and they could only be eliminated by shutting down the government. So a large number of mindless political trains arrived at the station at the same time at very high speeds.

Democrats will not destroy the safety net and Republicans will not raise revenues. Tea Party Republicans who now control their party refuse even token compromises with Democrats. So the mature nation of our founders, now divided sharply between red and blue (as the result of calculated gerrymandering at the state level), has produced a government incapable of governing.

Some decades from now, future generations will look back on all this with wonder. "What were they thinking?" they will ask. An accurate history will reveal that we were not thinking. Or, rather, we were thinking like adolescents. We wanted tax cuts and a balanced budget. We wanted to fight wars but not pay for them. We wanted to eliminate government programs except for those programs that benefited particular individuals or groups. We wanted high-wage jobs but did not want to pay for an educated and healthy workforce that could get to those jobs on public transportation. We wanted to burn more coal and gas but have clean air. And so it goes.

In his powerfully perceptive Pulitzer Prize–winning book, *People of Paradox*, Professor Michael Kammen writes: "We have tended to hold contradictory ideas in suspension and ignore the intellectual and behavioral consequences of such 'doublethink.'"

Long after economic catastrophes such as sequestration and refusal to pay our bills by rejecting a higher debt limit, there is the hope that future generations will think more clearly about political ideas that are too good to be true. Because they always are.

In the absence of founding principles and long-term strategies, politics has always been an attractive playground for myth. Myths play a central role as metaphors in many world religions according to Joseph Campbell. In *The Hero with a Thousand Faces* and *The Power of Myth*, he studied the world mythologies, found common themes in a wide variety of cultures, and reached a startling conclusion: Myths, he said, come from dreams and therefore people around the world have common dreams. It is a profound and still controversial insight for religion, psychology, and human culture. Students in all these fields continue to consider the power of myth.

Myths in politics, however, play a much different role. "Widely held but false idea" is one dictionary definition of "myth." For reasons that are still unclear, myths abound in recent American political history. Perhaps the most glaring and consequential one was the myth that Iraq under Saddam Hussein possessed weapons of mass destruction.

There are other cases in point—that Barack Obama is a Muslim born in Kenya and therefore not an American citizen. These are myths, yet they are widely believed in certain circles. Poor people are poor by choice—a classic myth. A rising tide lifts all boats—much more true when we were an industrial society and manufacturing products created jobs. Much less true when the economic tide is one of finance and money manipulation that lifts the gilded yachts but not the rowboats of the rest of us. Jobs are not created when crackpot financial schemes make hedge fund managers rich. Thus, the rising tide lifting all boats is a myth.

Myths in politics are dangerous. In an important speech at Yale University during the Cold War, John F. Kennedy said: "For the great enemy of the truth is very often not the lie—deliberate, contrived, and dishonest—but the myth—persistent, persuasive, and unrealistic. Too often we hold fast to the clichés of our forebears. We subject all facts to a prefabricated set of interpretations. We enjoy the comfort of opinion without the discomfort of thought." He was speaking of the myths on both sides that perpetuated the Cold War in dangerous ways.

More than fifty years later, no assessment comes closer to

describing much of our current political world. Reason and fact are sacrificed to opinion and myth. Demonstrable false-hoods are circulated and recycled as fact. Narrow-minded opinion refuses to be subjected to thought and analysis. Too many Americans now subject events to a prefabricated set of interpretations, usually provided by a biased media source. The myth is more comfortable than the often difficult search for truth. When established scientific facts, such as climate change, clash with myth, then people simply deny the science or demonize the scientist. New forms of Puritan witch-hunting are never far below the surface.

If this strange world was the product of mere laziness, it might be understandable. But today's political myths are more perverse. They are a conscious hiding place from a changing, challenging, and often uncomfortable new world. Globaliza-tion, immigration, and cultural and racial diversity are threat-ening and frightening to many who wish to freeze their formerly comfortable world in time and prevent any change.

Myths that have no basis in truth, or that do not operate as metaphors for religious truth, eventually fade away with the passing of those who perpetuate them and in the face of real-ity and fact. But the most dangerous myths create demons where none exist, the demons being anyone who disagrees with the mythmakers. In the meantime, however, such myths serve not only to delude the deniers but also to frustrate the Jeffersonian belief in the progress of the human mind.

Myths prevail in political vacuums, and four decades ago the Democratic Party permitted a vacuum of ideas to form. With Franklin Roosevelt, the Democratic Party became the party of both social justice and internationalism. But when the American economy hit a plateau in the mid to late 1970s, the Democrats did not present a coherent response.

The political party responsible for constructing the American social safety net, the Democratic Party, has always understood that this social contract could only be met if sufficient financial resources were available and that those resources, in the form of tax revenues, must come from an expanding economy. The World War II economy, fueled by extraordinary spending by the U.S. government, and the post–World War II economy covering the three decades from 1945 to 1975 produced more or less continued growth when the Greatest Generation returned to create families, buy houses, and work at new jobs.

But the mid-1970s brought a host of new economic realities: Cheap energy ended when the Organization of the Petroleum Exporting Countries (OPEC) tightened its grip on the oil market; the economy began to stagnate and the income of middle-class families plateaued; foreign competition in steel, autos, and textiles hit our shores; health care costs began to skyrocket; and a large cohort of the Greatest Generation began to retire to claim their share of entitlement programs. Added to this were the demands on the federal treasury to finance the Cold War and the Vietnam War. And, finally, the Johnson Great Society commitments greatly expanded the safety net to the poor of all races.

The net effect of these trains arriving at the station all at once was to call the Democrats' social contract into question. There were few economists and social analysts who could suggest a new system for financing New Deal and Great Society commitments, no Franklin Roosevelt to produce a long-term road map, and too few brain trusters capable of creating an economic vision to respond to this host of new realities.

A new generation of Democrats arrived on the political scene in the 1970s. We were faced with three options: one, hold fast to the New Deal faith and hope that taxpayers confronted with a number of economic constraints would continue to pay an increasing share of their incomes to finance it; two, shift the Democratic base to an ill-defined center with program cuts, especially to welfare for the poor, and some tax relief; or three, use new global realities to increase the size of the U.S. economic pie and provide sufficient middle-class economic security to finance the social safety net.

Democratic political representatives of the Greatest Generation by and large stayed the New Deal course, and many were defeated in the 1970s and '80s. In the 1990s the Democratic boomer generation came to power promoting the second option, and it and the nation benefited greatly from the new U.S. technology sector. The few of us who advocated the third option did not have the opportunity to try to structure a new economic and political base.

What might that have looked like? First: resisting protectionist pressures. This approach would have actively engaged the United States in global competition. Our competitive edge was, and in many respects still is, in high-value-added manufacturing such as specialty steels, new energy sources, and state-of-the-art transportation systems. Our advantage was then, and to a high degree still is, new technologies, especially in information and communications. Today we can add advanced medical technologies as well.

Second: As is now a common theme but was less so two or three decades ago, we could have had a national technology policy composed of educational incentives in all the sciences, math, and physics. We also should have substantially stimulated the national laboratory system, both public and private, to engage in advanced research in everything from energy to new materials to communications to medicine to environmental sciences. In sum, the transition of our economic base from manufacturing to information should have been the product of national policy, not random happenstance.

A third factor of the twenty-first-century policy foundation that could have been laid in the 1970s and '80s was a new post–Cold War foreign policy that identified more closely with the most fragile democratic movements in the postcolonial Third World that broke with anti-Communist dictators and left behind the stale "the enemy of my enemy is my friend" policy of the Cold War. Instead, we too often clung to undemocratic oligarchs who resisted democratic aspirations but who received our approval by being steadfastly anti-Communist.

A fourth unexplored dimension of an alternative Democratic platform was military reform, the comprehensive preparation of our force structures, weapons programs, officer training and promotion systems, and combat unit structures for the conflicts of the twenty-first century rather than those of the past. We could and should have begun two or three decades ago to prepare for the low-intensity conflicts of the future instead of the nation-state wars of past centuries. This would have meant fewer nuclear aircraft-carrier task groups, big bomber wings, and large army divisions and more special forces equipped with new technologies (robots, drones, surveillance systems, and so forth) to deal with threats that resembled those of the eleventh century more than those of the twentieth.

These four elements, and a wide variety of other options, were available to lay the base for an economy with increased opportunity, and thus security, for the middle class. And that economy could have provided the revenues required to meet our social obligations to those now increasingly left behind. In the absence of such a plan, we instead experimented with supply-side tax cuts that, though tried repeatedly, have failed to produce long-term investment and growth, with the deregulation of the financial sector that produced deeply flawed financial instruments good only for massive bonuses and the near collapse of the U.S. economy, and with two wars that were fought with forces unprepared for low-tech, unconventional insurgencies.

Even bad ideas will prevail in a political vacuum. And the Democratic Party, the party not only of the left but also of the future through progressive innovation and experimentation, permitted that vacuum to exist at a crucial point in our recent history. The nation now finds itself trying to dig out from the consequences of near collapse while searching for the resources required for global competition and economic integration.

Getting back on our feet fully and meeting the demands for political and economic leadership while meeting the humanitarian needs of a civilized society will require a renewed confidence in our political leadership, in the soundness of our currency, and, most of all, in ourselves. But signs of this renewal are scarce and prospects are not promising.

Political corruption, poverty, crime, the expediency of security, and the pursuit of dubious ideas continue to spotlight the gap between promise and performance. The ideal of the American Republic still shines brightly and attracts the fondest hopes of those excited by its principles. If Americans truly believe that others should follow us, our deeds must match our words. And to achieve this, our society requires serious repair.

Having spotlighted four principal arenas where the gap

between promise and deed is greatest, we must now consider the necessary steps toward achieving the Republic of Conscience and Principle.

G iven renewed investment in the private sector, continued innovation in government and private laboratories, a rebuilt public education system, simpler and fairer taxes, dramatic action on climate protection, and international cooperation on confinement of conflict, the United States will experience economic growth and opportunity, and become increasingly secure. On the plane of everyday living, therefore, we will continue to be envied and have a certain respect from many people around the world. But is that enough?

There is something more than the envy of an economic system that two-thirds of Americans enjoy. There is respect for our principles and ideals, a respect built on something greater than consumerism and materialism. That respect is moral authority.

In America's case, moral authority is based on living up to our proclaimed ideals and principles. That means achieving genuine equality for all. It means a social safety net that leaves no elderly, young, or poor person in poverty. It means an accessible, transparent, and honest political and electoral system open to all. It means economic opportunity for those able to work. It means food, medicine, and shelter for all Americans. It means honest and open dealings with all nations of goodwill.

Most of all, it means strong laws strongly enforced that disentangle interest groups from the lobbying industry and both of these entities from campaign finances. And it means security policies that protect our nation without violating our Constitutionally protected rights.

We will be well along the hard road in search of a unique destiny when governmental decisions are based on the national interest. For the national interest is separate from the massive hodgepodge of private interests. And it transcends generations. We will know we are serious about our ideals and principles when generational accountability, our responsibility to bequeath a better nation to future generations, guides our most important decisions.

We the People of the United States, in Order to form a more perfect Union, establish Justice, insure domestic Tranquility, provide for the common defence, promote the general Welfare, and secure the Blessings of Liberty to ourselves and our Posterity, do ordain and establish this Constitution for the United States of America.

This preamble to our Constitution sets out our goals as the founders saw them. But they made it clear for all time that these goals were not only for the current generation but they were equally guiding goals for "our Posterity."

THE REPUBLIC OF OUR FOUNDERS

Our founders were not impractical dreamers. They emphatically understood what they were doing when they created this nation. A careful reading of our Declaration of Independence, our Constitution, *The Federalist Papers*, the mountain of letters they all wrote to each other, and the Constitutional debates can lead to no other conclusion than that they intended this nation to be what they designed it to be. They were individuals of conviction, but also of practical conviction.

Our founders intentionally set high standards for governing this nation. But even more important, they believed we would maintain our unique identity *only if* we lived up to those standards. "A republic, if you can keep it" was Benjamin Franklin's famous description of what they were up to at the Constitutional Convention. Our structures and beliefs were not unachievable dreams; they were necessary to ensure our survival.

Those who created the United States employed the language, principles, and ideals of the republic. They were, virtually to a man, students of the ancient Greek and Roman republics, and thoroughly familiar with the classical political works from both eras as well as how those works made their way into the thinking of the English and Scottish Enlightenment that provided the intellectual foundation for our founding documents and government systems.

In *The Federalist* No. 39, James Madison gave his understanding of the republic that was being created: "A government which derives all its powers directly or indirectly from the great body of people, and is administered by persons holding their offices during pleasure, for a limited period, or during good behavior. It is *essential* to such a government that it be derived from the great body of the society, not from an inconsiderable proportion, or a favoured class of it."

They knew also that republics throughout history had been relatively small entities—primarily city-states—whether ancient Athens, pre-imperial Rome, Venice, or the Swiss cantons—and that the republican ideal had not flourished in the Middle Ages until it was resurrected in the sixteenth century by Niccolò Machiavelli, who made it one of his more positive gifts to the Age of Enlightenment.

Faced with uniting thirteen more or less autonomous republics or commonwealths under a single central government, the Constitutionalists found instruction in the writings of Montesquieu for the creation of a federated republic, and that concept underwrote their unique effort to create a republic on a scope and scale without precedent in human history. Given that no conceivable forum could hold even the propertied males within the American population of roughly three million in 1789, elected representation offered the solution for a government of, for, and by the people.

Even a cursory reading of the Constitutional debates and *The Federalist Papers* reveals the clear understanding of virtually all those participating in the creation of the United States that they were involved in a novel experiment, one that could only be sustained beyond their own lifetimes by the adherence to fundamental notions of society and government. Their collective pragmatism made them understand that those notions would have to be applied to the evolving realities of future eras. But their collective idealism made them believe that substantial deviance from the principles and ideals they built into this new governing system would inevitably produce a different nation from the one they intended. Their genius was the conscious knowledge that they were creating a new approach to civilized society, one that required civic virtue and citizen participation if their posterity was to maintain it.

The founders were deeply concerned with corruption—personal interests over the common good—because it undermined core constitutional principles. A powerful motivation for America's revolution was the belief that the English constitution (unwritten) had become irredeemably corrupt because that corruption had drained the popular spirit that underwrote the constitution. In his majestic *The Creation of the American Republic, 1776–1787*, the eminent historian Gordon S. Wood makes the case that times change and republics must adapt, but that they must constantly renew their dedication to the principles upon which they were founded: "Had not Machiavelli and [Algernon] Sidney both written that 'all human Constitutions are subject to Corruption and must perish, unless they are *timely renewed* by reducing them to their first Principles'?"

The dilemma in early twenty-first-century American politics mirrors the conflict in late seventeenth- and early eighteenth-century England between the Court and the Country. Because that struggle engaged the minds of some of the best political thinkers of that time in both England and Scotland, and because those thinkers were well known to America's founders, the contest between Court and Country would make its way into the debates surrounding the founding of the American Republic.

In simple terms, the Court was the center of power in

post-Reformation England and the Country represented an emerging society of professional gentry increasingly disinclined to let traditional power structures dictate the terms of their personal and community lives. In the countryside was an emerging generation of educated, property-owning gentry sufficiently independent and self-directed to resist the dictates of privilege and the impositions of governance of their lives by distant rulers.

In more philosophical terms, the issues of interests versus virtue were mirrored in this struggle. The Court represented interests, including estates, money, and power, and the Country represented the classical values of civic virtue dating from ancient Athens and Rome. In political terms, the Court was concerned with the preservation and perpetuation of its interests through the exercise of its powers, while the Country wished to see the restoration of the ideal of virtue in governance, placing the interests of the commonwealth ahead of the interests of the Court.

In very general terms this contest made its way across the Atlantic as the colonies began to organize their resistance to the English Court, and they did so in philosophical terms by restoring the ideal of civic virtue. It is by no means accidental that America's founders were scholars or at least students of the classical republican era in Athens and Rome, and were very well versed in the writings and the concepts of the theorists of the republic. This accounts for their almost universal distrust of concentrated wealth and power, the Republicans more than the Federalists, as reflective of the English Court, and strongly confirmed their deeply held belief in citizen virtue as the foundation of the government they hoped to create.

For James Madison and the others, systems of checks and balances were necessary to prevent one branch of government from overpowering the others, but even more to prevent the kind of concentration of power that might replicate the Court system from which they had so recently separated. But Madison also saw checks and balances as the bulwark against corruption in the almost inevitable appearance of factions and interest.

Professor Gordon Wood summarizes the dilemma: "When the American Whigs described the English nation and government as eaten away by 'corruption,' they were in fact using a technical term of political science, rooted in the writings of classical antiquity, made famous by Machiavelli, developed by the classical republicans of seventeenth-century England, and carried into the eighteenth century by nearly everyone who laid claim to knowing anything about politics. And for England it was a pervasive corruption, not only dissolving the original political principles by which the constitution was balanced, but, more alarming, sapping the very spirit of the people by which the constitution was ultimately sustained." Our Revolutionary War was justified as much as anything by the widespread corruption seen to have overtaken the English system.

And that concern for the corruption of republican virtue by interests was expressed even as the earliest generation of founders, such as John Adams and Richard Henry Lee, laid the groundwork for an American Republic that would resist what they saw as a "Design" afoot by "a joynt Combination of political and Commercial Men . . . to get the Trade, the Wealth, the Power and the Government of America into their own Hands." The history of republics was the constant struggle between those interested in power and wealth and those virtuous patriots who placed the commonwealth above their own fortunes. They would be appalled today at the measure by which their hopes have been dashed.

All this is relevant in twenty-first-century America because the seat of government in Washington, regardless of the political party in power, has become the new Court. The permanent political class that occupies the capital has concentrated power and wealth in itself, and the clash of political fortunes carried out in national elections is not between the Court and the Country, but between which political faction will dominate, for the time being, the Court.

Among many other fears the founders had about concentrated wealth and power in control of government was the perpetuation of small numbers of families and the retinues of retainers, supporters, and place seekers that surrounded them.

It is in the nature of interests to protect themselves, and what better way to do so than to negotiate comfortable arrangements with a few political families to attain and maintain political office.

Though the Adams family may have come to represent a dynasty of sorts—though almost entirely through merit—Washington, Madison, and Jefferson, among many others, retired from office and departed from the capital without seeking to leave behind a successor generation to perpetuate name, policy, and powerful networks.

The intricate lobbying system, now so highly evolved that virtually every lobbying interest has both former Republican and Democratic officeholders in its ranks, guarantees that, regardless of who wins an election, the same influence, the same exorbitant fee structures, and the same interests will be protected and promoted. The outrage at the national government's bailout of gigantic Wall Street banks has its echoes in the clash between Court and Country three centuries before.

The current stalemate in government has deep ideological roots in the struggle between the pragmatic liberalism of Franklin Roosevelt and the conservatism of Robert Taft (although Ronald Reagan is the reigning conservative hero, he merely jumped on a conservative train that had principles that long predated him). These ideologies represent the "factions" so dreaded by the founders. But our current impasse also has much deeper roots in the three-centuries-old struggle between Court and Country that our founders inherited from England. This book argues that we will not witness a restoration of the republic until the power of the present Court's interests, alternatively shared by both political parties and their retinues, is replaced by the civic virtue of the Country and by the timely renewal of the first principles of our Constitution.

Underlying the bitter, often furious, clash between parties is a contest for power and the control of interests, wealth, and fortune first recognized in its most elementary form by Machiavelli. We consider ourselves higher on the moral scale by degrees of magnitude over the instructions on the use of political power dispersed by the wily Florentine. But, in the harsh light of twenty-first-century reality, his blunt recognition of the uses of power and interest in the elementary republic of his day still rings true.

By placing our current dilemma in this historical context, we might form a clearer picture of how deep and divisive this contest has been over the years predating our birth as a nation and how deeply rooted in political thought this struggle has been. It is not new. This is, as Harry Truman once said, simply the history we do not know.

Of course, it matters to the Country, too often only on the margins, which of the two dominant parties prevail. But for the possessors of wealth, power, influence, and interest, it

matters little if at all. A tax loophole here, a government sub-
sidy there. This is all handled behind the scenes by the en-
trenched lobbying industry that serves the interests.

This industry has its historical roots in the acolytes of the
Court—the courtiers, who made themselves available to those
sharing the Court's powers to facilitate its purposes and protect its interests. Twenty-first-century courtiers also include the
growing permanent political class that goes in and out of office
depending on electoral fortunes. Out of office, this policy class,
as distinct (usually) from the lobbying class, finds refuge in
the many think tanks and policy centers, many of which were
established in recent years as refuges for those permanent
officeholders who find themselves temporarily out of office.

Though most of the policy centers and think tanks make
general disclosures of their sources of financing, including
press disclosures of foreign financial investments, their good-
government agendas form a context for those who have come
to Washington, often at a young age, and never intend to
leave. Administrations of both parties in recent decades have
simply recycled the officeholders from previous administrations of those parties. Thus, among the courtiers is a class of
policy makers promoting the same policy agendas and using
the same Rolodex networks of previous administrations.

In terms of national leadership, this same pattern may
explain why those qualifying seem to come from fewer and
fewer families, as if leadership required preclearance by the

Court to qualify for consideration. In a nation of more than 300 million people, surely there are those capable of governing whose relatives have not paved the way. And even when an outlier such as Barack Obama suddenly breaks this mold, he finds himself surrounded by an administration in part prepositioned by an early Court.

Thus, the courtiers themselves are a bulwark against innovative thinking and imaginative ideas to address new realities. They are in service of power and interest and the protection of the status quo. In this way the Court guarantees its own survival and permanence. Little wonder that those in the Country, suspicious of those intricate, often hidden networks, find themselves increasingly at odds with "Washington," the modern version of the Court. The nation meanwhile is offered the stability of power and interest structures at the cost of innovation, imagination, and creative governance.

It seems self-evident that Congress, the elected representatives of the people who are sovereign, should counterbalance the Court, if not force it to diffuse. But the conversion of our nation into solidly Democratic and Republican states and congressional districts (about 80 percent of each brought about by gerrymandering and coalition manipulation) has rendered Congress incapable of breaking down the Court system. Indeed, with the transition of so many former senators and congresspersons and their families into the lobbying industry so central to the Court, Congress itself has become an adjunct of the

Washington Court and party to the conversion of our nation into one of interests rather than one of civic virtue as envisioned by our founders.

Since late seventeenth-century England, the hallmarks of the Court have been place, patronage, privilege, and prerogative. This coinage in the realm of the early twenty-first-century American Court prevails even to this day.

To see how far astray we have gone, contrast our current corrupt politics of special interests with Gordon Wood's summary of our early American founders: "The sacrifice of individual interests to the greater good of the whole formed the essence of republicanism and comprehended for Americans the idealistic goal of their Revolution." Civic virtue was required to sustain the Republic created by its early founders. The "willingness of the individual to sacrifice his private interests for the good of the community—such patriotism or love of country—the eighteenth century termed 'public virtue.'"

What would the founders make of a nation now much larger in population and area than the one for which they devised a government? They clearly knew their new nation would expand, the more visionary among them imagining it becoming much greater than the others did. Some lived to see new roads extending west and canal systems running north and south. The Louisiana Purchase and the resolution of the ownership of the Floridas gave a clear indication of what lay ahead for "our posterity."

But the system of government laid down in the Constitution could accommodate a nation of much greater scale only if its principles were constantly revisited and renewed to take into account changing times and evolving events.

The scale of the Republic, larger at its founding than any in human history, would continue to take into account elected representation from the original colonies, then the states, and then the new territories that were admitted as the Union grew. But it would require a reflective Jefferson, late in life following his presidency, to ponder the downside of dependence on representation and the loss of citizen engagement in self-government, and thus civic virtue, caused by an expanding United States.

In a renewed correspondence with John Adams, among several others, Jefferson expressed concern that a republic of representation might lead to citizen alienation. In this case he anticipated America in the late twentieth and early twenty-first centuries. Though he did not advocate revisiting the Constitution, he did urge identification and empowerment of what he variously called "ward" or "elementary" republics, local township governments in which participating citizens would collectively resolve issues peculiar to them alone, such as the performance of their local public schools, but which they might have in common with other communities of equal dimension.

Reflecting his ever-imaginative approach to most human endeavors, Jefferson stated in a letter to John Adams in February

1796: "This I hope will be the age of experiments in government." Later, in a letter to Joseph C. Cabell in 1816, seven years after leaving the presidency, Jefferson laid out his elaborate scheme of government: "The way to have good and safe government, is not to trust it all to one [level], but to divide it among the many, distributing to every one exactly the functions he is competent to. Let the national government be entrusted with the defence of the nation, and its foreign and federal relations; the State governments with the civil rights, laws, police, and administration of what concerns the State generally; the counties with the local concerns of the counties, and each ward direct the interests within itself. It is by dividing and subdividing these republics from the great national one down through all its subordinations, until it ends in the administration of every man's farm by himself; by placing under every one what his own eye may superintend, that all will be done for the best."

When cities began to burn in the 1960s following the assassinations of Martin Luther King, Jr., and John and Robert Kennedy and the dramatic rise of the civil rights movement, the Johnson administration enacted community development programs that placed considerable administrative powers with local governments, both at the municipal and neighborhood levels. This was followed by something called the New Federalism in the Nixon era in which existing and new federal social mandates were funded by block grants administered by state governments. Serious social problems were acknowledged, but so was a sense of alienation and loss of empowerment. Administrative power was devolved, but under federal mandates and guidelines. During that period, few went so far as to argue for Jefferson's elementary republics.

Arguably, however, local—"ward"—republics can superintend local public schools, administer public assistance programs according to the needs of the community, and even, through local National Guard units, play a role in homeland security. Some twenty-first-century variation on this theme deserves consideration, if nothing else than to address the lament that "I don't make a difference" and "Washington doesn't care what I think."

The issue is a real one. If the gap between who we think we are as a nation and how we behave as a nation is to be reduced by resorting to the principles upon which our nation was founded, and one of those principles is the need for civic virtue and citizen participation, then reconsideration of citizen power within a complex layered system of government is timely.

Jefferson may or may not have been speculating wide of the mark with the notion of elementary (local) republics, but at least he was addressing a real issue, one raised by the disparity between the republican ideal and how it was adapted to early American realities. And, to my knowledge, he was the only founder to do so.

If Machiavelli, among other early theorists of the republic, observed that "timely renewal" of the first principles of a republican constitution was the only way to prevent its inevitable corruption by time and change, then the Jefferson concern, if not also the Jefferson remedy, is worth our serious consideration.

Much of the current unease in the land involves citizen alienation from "Washington," but it is also a latent but powerful sense that we are adrift, adrift not simply on a sea of globalization and international competition nor lost in a jungle of primitive terrorism, but adrift from our founding principles. We come closest to the ideal our founders established for renewal of our Republic during times of justifiable war abroad or threat of economic depression at home, but we find it difficult to unite around a positive agenda of renewal of our political faith absent a foreign or domestic crisis. Indeed, we are as far from uniting around a national renewal of principle as we have ever been.

Harsh ideology has replaced the interests of the national community, and special interest corruption pervades the permanent political class in Washington. The insistence that America be governed according to the dictates of a minority, and a small minority at that, has ground consensus governance to a halt. The politics of stalemate prevail. Members of Congress are rewarded for blind and unquestioned opposition. Party and ideology routinely are placed before the national interest. Party leaders declare their sole purpose to be the defeat of a president of the United States elected twice by a majority of Americans. Under such conditions, the timely renewal of first principles required to assure the Republic's continued survival seems far removed from the counsel of our founders and the enlightened thinkers upon whom they depended.

We are envied for our standard of living. We are feared, sometimes even by our friends, for our military power. Many people are staggered by the immense wealth concentrated at the top of our society. Our movies and music are enjoyed and replicated worldwide. Those who have had the benefit of travel know, however, that in every country and every society there are thoughtful and humble people who respect the United States for the ideals upon which it was founded. In most cases they cling to the hope for a governing system for themselves based on the principles for which we stand.

The overwhelming majority of humans are suffering under systems of oligarchy, decaying colonial legacies, false nationalism, religious fanaticism, kleptocracies, ancient tribalisms, aging royalty, and every form of corruption conceivable. As our founders knew, human beings innately long for freedom, self-government, and respect.

Put forth out of "a decent respect for the opinions of mankind" 239 years ago in the Declaration of Independence and incorporated into a governing system in the Constitution twelve years later, our ideals distilled from the Enlightenment encompass human equality, unalienable rights, balanced and checked political power, majority rule that protects minority rights, free elections, representative government, religious and political freedom, and justice for all. Much more than most Americans realize, however, those same people who admire and respect these ideals keenly observe when we fail to live up to them.

Our founding documents avoid slavery and the rights of indigenous peoples. They do not authorize intervention in foreign nations whether for regime change or the promotion of our system of government. They most assuredly do not authorize us to be the arsenal or police force of the world. They warn against mixing religion and politics. They promote the progress, not the ignorance, of science.

We are an uneven and imperfect beacon for our ideals and principles. They are noble; they are just. But they must be lived up to in the conduct of our nation's business. We disappoint those who admire and respect us not when we experience economic downturn or when we misuse our military power but when we do not behave at home and abroad according to the standards we set for ourselves in our statements of principle.

Those who wrote and voted for the Declaration of Independence and the Constitution did not consider their ideals to be unrealistic or unachievable. The first two paragraphs of the Declaration of Independence and the preamble to the Constitution define a secular sacred scripture, a national political religion. But they are not dreamy, pie-in-the-sky rhetoric. The founders meant what they said and they pledged their lives, their fortunes, and their sacred honor to those achievable ideals.

Underlying all of it was the commonly held belief that good men (in those days) and women today would achieve a governing consensus to make the new experiment work on a day-to-day basis. They decried partisan ideology ("factions") and would be appalled at partisanship that opposes every initiative of a duly elected executive branch and that places the success of the party over the national interest.

If we still maintain even a shred of decent respect for the opinions of mankind, we will ask ourselves often how our current domestic politics and foreign policy appear to those around the world who look to our founding ideals for guidance and hope, who long to live in a nation that claims for its citizens the rights and protections our Declaration of Independence and Constitution embody.

We have much work still to do to live up to our principles and ideals, and we have a long way to travel. But if we continue with that effort, the opinions of mankind will reward us, and the respect of mankind will be ours.

A REPUBLIC WE
DID NOT KEEP

Remembering Benjamin Franklin's wise description of the political entity his and other founders' geniuses helped create should stimulate a national self-examination every few decades to ask ourselves how we are doing. At the present time, many Americans would say not very well.

The gap between belief and performance—who we believe ourselves to be and who we actually are in our conduct—has rarely been larger in our history. What created this disparity? Was there a single point of departure where we took the wrong fork in the road? What factors brought us to this point?

Rarely do great nations cast off their moorings as the result of a single cause. In the case of the United States, a number of major decisions were made from the middle of the twentieth century onward that have determined our course since. A few policy decisions were dramatic, but most were gradual if not imperceptible. Some of those trends related to America's role in the world. Others had to do with the management of our domestic political and economic structures and institutions.

THE NATIONAL SECURITY STATE

By accepting the burden of policing the world, the United States became a different country from the one originally founded.

In 1947 Congress passed and President Harry Truman signed the National Security Act. This sweeping legislation confirmed the United States as the dominant military power on Earth and set us on a course unprecedented in our history. A relatively small pre–World War II military became a large standing army and navy and the small prewar War Department became the Pentagon. A new fourth military service, the United States Air Force, was created. A permanent National Security Council was established by law. And, perhaps most consequential, a Central Intelligence Agency was created.

Far-flung military units deployed throughout Europe and Asia during World War II quickly became permanent U.S. military bases and they expanded throughout the Cold War. Naval fleets rotated on extended cruises in the major oceans of the world and long-range bombers carrying nuclear warheads were kept in the air. Soon they were joined by intercontinental strategic missiles with nuclear warheads, the entire nuclear arsenal eventually numbering in the tens of thousands of warheads.

A short decade later, the outgoing Republican President and Supreme Commander in World War II, Dwight Eisenhower, would warn the nation against the creation of a military-industrial complex. Too late.

Though Eisenhower's warning was concerned with the economic and political power of this complex, and rightly so, he might well have used the occasion to remind the American people of the universal opposition of their founders to standing armies. For a hallmark of republics throughout history was the suspicion of the temptation toward dictatorship that a permanent professional military force represented. It was not only a burden on the treasury of the republic, it was also an invitation to treachery, autocracy, and the sacrifice of freedom. From antiquity onward, professional standing armies were more often than not composed of mercenaries and soldiers of fortune, not citizens of the republic.

Much to the dismay of the anti-Federalists, the Constitution did provide for a small army and navy with a civilian as its commander in chief and a budget strictly controlled by the representatives of the people in Congress. And it was to be sent to war only by express authorization of the Congress, a Constitutional requirement made quaint in recent years by Congress's abdication of this responsibility and successive commanders in chief who usurped the authority to raise the sword when and where it suited their respective fancies. President Obama side-stepped this clear Constitutional mandate in unilaterally declaring some form of war on the Islamic State, a stateless nation. Then in February 2015, the president submitted to Congress a request for formal approval of military action against ISIS, and many who had previously urged him to escalate military deployments resisted going on record as formally authorizing it.

The overwhelming justification for this epic departure from our deeply felt founding principles was the perceived threat of Communism in Europe, Asia, and the developing postcolonial nations of the world. This Cold War framework for foreign and defense policy prevailed until the collapse of the Soviet Union virtually overnight in 1991. Under the banner of containing Communism, the Korean and Vietnam wars were fought at the cost of more than a hundred thousand American dead and tens of thousands of others among the wounded casualties. The financial costs to the taxpayers and the U.S. Treasury of waging these wars and maintaining an unprecedented permanent military establishment were astronomical.

History will take its own time in determining the degree to which the Communist threat reflected reality and warranted America's emergence as a permanent military superpower. Most certainly the actions of the United States prevented South Korea from falling to a harsh Communist dictatorship. But the dominoes predicted to topple in Southeast Asia after the fall of South Vietnam are still in place.

Virtually all the rest of the conflicts during the second half of the twentieth century were carried out in the back alleys of the world by the newly authorized and steadily expanding clandestine services. Initially created to collect secret intelligence, to analyze this intelligence for policy makers, and to convert those secrets into policy options, these agencies quickly went from the passing of money to agents to high-tech surveillance and then into the penetration of foreign governments and national borders and then into covert operations aimed at overthrowing those governments and eliminating "with extreme prejudice" anyone who got in the way, including uncooperative heads of state.

It is amazing how quickly one thing can lead to another not only in the fiction of spy thrillers but also in the all-too-real world. This became problematic when the issue of command and control emerged. Who was in charge? Who authorized these operations?

One school of thought, usually identified with the late Senator Frank Church, held that the CIA was a "rogue elephant" undertaking murder and mayhem at its own whim whenever and wherever it pleased. Another routine explanation came to be known as "plausible deniability," the ordering of a covert escapade by one president or another who suddenly knew nothing about it when it "blew back," that is, when it fell apart. Either way, successive Congresses knew nothing about any of it and were just as happy not to know.

Given the number of false and misleading stories and theories promoted by an army of self-appointed "experts" in the intelligence world, anyone commenting on that world must establish credentials. Mine go back half a century. My first job following law school graduation was in what is now known as the national security division of the United States Department of Justice. A decade later I was elected to the United States Senate and was almost immediately appointed to the Senate Select Committee to Study Governmental Operations with Respect to Intelligence Agencies, better known as the Church Committee after its chairman, Frank Church. One of the many reform recommendations of that committee in 1976 was to create a permanent Senate intelligence oversight committee, and I became a charter member of that committee. In addition, as a member of the Senate Armed Services Committee, I also had access to the highest level of military intelligence and cutting-edge weapons development.

Then, after leaving office in 1987, I was appointed cochairman, with the late Senator Warren Rudman, of the U.S. Commission on National Security for the Twenty-First Century in 1998. That commission warned the nation as early as 1999 and also in its final report in January 2001 that terrorists were going to attack the United States and that "Americans will die on American soil, possibly in large numbers." Neither the new Bush administration nor the press paid any attention.

Finally, today I am serving on and chairing committees in both the Department of State and the Department of Defense on national and international security matters, and both assignments require high-level clearances.

All of this is not by way of self-promotion but by way of establishing my qualifications to observe and comment on the role of intelligence in a democracy. For well before Edward Snowden, the trade-off between security and liberty in America had become problematic at best and perilous at worst.

Because of the Church Committee, we have congressional oversight of intelligence operations. It did not take all that long for the CIA, some would say predictably, to spy on the Senate Select Committee on Intelligence by hacking into committee computers to discover what the committee knew about CIA misdeeds including torture. In the meantime, its sister agency, the National Security Agency, has been vacuuming up tens of millions of electronic communications between and among American citizens in search of a terrorist needle. Questioned about the process for finding needles in haystacks, an experienced insider said: First you have to create a haystack.

One way or another, "intelligence" has preoccupied a few of us for most of our lives. In my case, it started with Watergate, followed by the Church Committee. Now it is Edward Snowden and the National Security Agency. Very few Americans dispute the need to collect and analyze information in most parts of the world. During the Cold War, intelligence told us whether the Soviet Union was preparing to launch missiles. During the age of terrorism, intelligence is meant to prevent hijacked airplanes from flying into tall buildings.

Intelligence becomes problematic when it targets Americans, contrary to the Constitution, and when it slides into covert operations. Even years after the end of the Cold War, the intelligence "community" continues to expand in size and budget, spreading into the gray area of consultants, which are very expensive private operations run by people who have not taken an oath to uphold and defend the Constitution.

Three hundred and thirty million Americans cannot vote on when to and when not to carry out a covert operation. After 9/11, there was little criticism of inserting covert operators into Tora Bora to capture or eliminate Osama bin Laden. But that operation was the tip of a very large iceberg that has encompassed government overthrows, regime changes, assassination plots, political subversions, and a host of other operations across the globe. Almost all of these were and are traceable to the operations directorate of the CIA.

The vast majority of us want the CIA to collect and analyze information as effectively and accurately as humanly possible. When the world becomes peaceful, we will no longer need this activity. Since that is not going to happen anytime soon, the American people and their elected representatives must face some hard choices. In addition to information collection and intelligence, do we want our government spying on us, and do we want covert operators carrying out quasi-military operations (let alone building secret prisons) in a wide variety of countries around the world?

These questions do seem repetitive, but that is because they are still not resolved. And they won't be resolved until the American people make it clear where they stand on these two key questions. Philosophers would call these questions existential, that is, they define who we are and who we believe ourselves to be.

Of these two key questions, surveillance of Americans is the more troublesome. Where our security is clearly at risk, covert operations should be undertaken by the military. These are military missions and the only reason we use CIA operatives to carry them out rather than military special forces is a pathetic fiction: If they blow back, we (the president) can deny they were officially authorized or deny the operation in question was an act of war. In the large majority of covert operations gone wrong, the elephant did not go rogue on its own; it did so on orders from the White House.

Technology is making protection of Fourth Amendment rights against search and seizure more complex. Tapping into massive electronic servers and hoovering up all phone calls and messages then filtering them for evildoers is easier than identifying the evildoers and limiting the surveillance to them. But our Constitution clearly instructs our government not to do that. The so-called FISA (Foreign Intelligence Surveillance

Act) courts have not proved adequate to prevent unconstitutional mass surveillance.

This elusive discussion is usually summarized as a struggle between security and liberty. It is deeper than that. It is a dilemma that defines us as a nation. It penetrates to the heart of our unique Constitutional principles and the identity of America. The national security state created by the National Security Act of 1947 has leaped its Constitutional bounds and threatens to redefine our nature, our purpose, and our character.

At the very least, the creation of the national security state in 1947 fundamentally altered the way the nation created by our founders defended itself. Though they created a small standing army and navy, they left the burden of homeland defense to the militia mentioned in three different parts of the Constitution. They provided for the arming of that militia in the Second Amendment to the Constitution. Like republics from Athens onward, the protection of the republic rested with the citizen-soldier, not with a professional army they so feared.

Since World War II, the United States has been incredibly fortunate in the professionalism of our military officer corps and its strict adherence to civilian command. This is a tribute to the highest commitment to democratic ideals. However, the consideration remains. Are we still in a world requiring us to maintain the size of the military establishment of nearly seven decades ago or have circumstances changed?

Nation-state wars, so characteristic of the past three and a half centuries, are declining rapidly. That does not mean they are impossible. It does mean that the cost of acquisition of territory or the promotion of ideology is no longer acceptable. Instead, we are in an era of unconventional, irregular conflict requiring special forces who do not need nuclear aircraft-carrier task groups, large long-range bomber wings, and big army divisions. Thus, this might be a moment in history to consider an approach to security more compatible with the principles and ideals of our founders.

But such a calculation would require the United States and its leaders to do something they have not proved very adept at: anticipating events and taking protective actions in preparation for harmful outcomes. Much of this reluctance to anticipate is rooted in the continuing suspicion of government. It is difficult for conservatives in particular to entrust government agencies with anticipatory actions when they instinctively distrust the size and power of government. Resistance to "centralized planning" caused suspicion of anticipatory preparation. (This, in part, explains the reluctance of the George W. Bush administration to heed warnings of inevitable terrorist attacks.)

In a world increasingly composed of stateless nations, nonstate actors, tribes, clans, gangs without governments or borders, ethnic nationalists, and religious fanatics, events—especially dangerous events—have escaped the bounds of rational behavior or even questionable national interest. This makes future security both more unpredictable and, at the same time, more important to anticipate. This dichotomy seems contradictory and it is. And it does justify intelligence capabilities focused on unpredictable actors who use novel methods of destruction such as converting commercial airliners into suicidal missiles.

Post 9/11, the exploding Cold War intelligence world has relied on massive communications-collecting hoovers to construct haystacks of data in which to look for needles. But it is now common knowledge that the data collected is so vast that billion-dollar storage warehouses are being built in the hope that someone someday will get around to sorting through it in the hope of finding a needle. Of course, by then it will be too late.

Thus, as warfare is retreating to the barbaric age of the assassins in the eleventh century (presuming the use of weapons of mass destruction is not even more barbaric), it is apparent that the most effective means of finding the intelligence needle will remain the most difficult. Human intelligence (HUMINT, as the acronym goes) elicited by one agent from another by means of wine, women, song, and money still holds the greatest promise of catastrophe avoidance. It is cheap; it requires spectacular skill—and luck—and it is dangerous. But it might avoid future 9/11s and it might have avoided the first one.

This John le Carré approach to security, whether in from

the cold or not, has the added advantage of better protecting the Constitutional rights and freedoms of the American people. Presuming we have sufficiently matured to avoid future "Red scares" and the witch hunts of the 1950s, and to not take the easy course of seeking the terrorist devil in our midst, our intelligence services might well be redirected away from much of their current fascination with high technologies to the more difficult but more effective human touch.

If so, we will have marked a major restoration of the democratic republic of our founders, one whose security is provided by more appropriately sized and more effective military forces that are deployed after due regard for Constitutional mandates from the people through their elected representatives and by an intelligence collection and analysis capability that uses clandestine operations only under the most dire circumstances and only against the murky groups that wish us ill and intend to act on that wish.

The national security state has yet to come to grips with the evolution of fourth-generation warfare (after line and column, fire and movement, and maneuver and infiltration). Characteristic of conflicts of the past two or three decades, this new (yet old) warfare is insurgent, irregular, decentralized, unconventional, and low intensity.

Because we remained on a semi-war footing throughout the Cold War, when a handful of terrorists wearing civilian clothes hijacked airplanes and flew them into buildings, we declared "war on terrorism." But some argued that this was not warfare, this was criminal behavior, and attacking dispersed bands of al-Qaeda and the Taliban in the Afghan mountains with large-scale military forces (and even more so in Iraq) was a mistake of strategy and tactics.

Following the disappearance of the bipolar world of the twentieth century and the erosion of nation-state sovereignty, violence by stateless nations—usually lumped under the category of terrorism—has repeatedly surfaced. Russia's suppression of Chechnyan nationalism brought this kind of violence to Moscow. The United States' stationing of troops in Saudi Arabia during Gulf War I eventually led to the rise of al-Qaeda and the 9/11 attacks on America that followed earlier attacks on U.S. embassies in Africa and the Marine barracks in Lebanon. Somali pirates attacked international maritime traffic off the Horn of Africa. Israel expands settlements and Palestinians retaliate with rockets. Separatists and ultranationalists employ violence to demonstrate their anger.

Following the 9/11 attacks on the United States, we invaded Afghanistan to seek vengeance on al-Qaeda and to destabilize the Taliban, an organization we had supported in its fight against the Soviet occupation. Then, against facts and logic, we chose to confine that mission, some think on the brink of success, to wage war against Iraq, which had not previously attacked us.

In the process of both undertakings, we captured prisoners, imprisoned many in "black" prisons operated by other nations on our behalf, tortured some, and placed several hundred in the partially abandoned facilities at Guantanamo Bay, Cuba. They were labeled "enemy combatants," a category invented for the occasion. Though our president had declared "war on terrorism," we did not recognize them as warriors or prisoners of war. We refused to do so because there were several Geneva Conventions on War that would have required us to pursue policies regarding the treatment of prisoners incompatible with what we were doing, including repatriation of prisoners upon the conclusion of hostilities.

It seems not to have occurred to either the George W. Bush administration or most members of Congress that this war might not end at any identifiable future date. Thus, we had a significant number of "enemy combatants" that we did not know what to do with. That awkward political can was kicked down the road for the future Obama administration to deal with. And it has done so not by closing the Guantanamo prisoner camp as promised but by gradually depleting the prison population through arm-twisting foreign governments to take the prisoners off our hands. There is every reason to believe that the next administration will inherit this ugly problem whether it wants to or not.

Future generations will study this matter as a classic NIMBY—"not in my backyard." Rather than simply shipping Guantanamo "enemy combatants" off to "supermax" prisons across the United States, the Obama administration, within days of taking office, sought to reason with members of Congress in whose states those prisons were located and it was met by teeth-gritting resistance.

Even before the advent of the "enemy combatant" era, a few of us were advocating a different course, indeed a different philosophy, in dealing with those accused of plotting or carrying out terrorist activities. They were and are criminals. and should be dealt with as criminals, not as warriors or with some vague enemy combatant status. We have a criminal justice system. To date, a significant number of those accused of terrorism have been tried and convicted in civilian, not military, courts of law.

Treating those who plot death to civilian Americans as warriors or even pseudowarriors is a serious mistake. They are criminals. Possession of a stitched-up flag and an AK-47 does not make you a warrior. Using that weapon makes you a criminal. Even declaring yourself to have a capital in Iraq, as the Islamic State has done, does not confer warrior status on your combatants. Any ragtag billionaire can buy an island, raise a flag, and declare himself a nation. Nevertheless, international recognition is required before he actually becomes one.

We are in this conundrum as much as anything because the George W. Bush administration did not trust the courts of the United States. And in many cases the courts were not trusted because they required evidence of violations of the laws of the United States. The claim was made that much of that evidence was classified. In a few cases that might be true. Even more persuasive, however, is the notion that there was insufficient evidence to convict a so-called enemy combatant who may have been pulled from a hidey-hole in an Afghan desert on an unconfirmed allegation by his brother-in-law or opposing tribesman that he was a terrorist.

There is yet another lesson in the complex legacies left by expedient actions here. Declare war, capture prisoners, invent a new status for them, lock them up in a remote location outside the jurisdiction of the U.S. courts—and let the next administration worry about it.

Would not serious adults governing a mature nation take a different approach and inspire a debate on the nature of terrorism and the people who carry it out? Terrorism is a method, not a philosophy or an ideology. By and large, terrorists do not wear uniforms and do not represent a government with a capital. They violate the rules of civilized warfare, attack noncombatants, torture and behead their kidnapped prisoners, and behave essentially like drug cartels in Mexico and Central America. If that is not criminal behavior, what is?

If you get categories wrong, you get responses wrong. The rise of the stateless nation, whether it is a radical fundamentalist group, a drug cartel, or a black-market arms bazaar, confronts a world that was used to having organized violence under national flags with a new disorganized violence, that is to say, violence not carried out by one nation against another.

The so-called Islamic State offers a new paradigm. It does not claim a capital or a form of internal government. It occupies territories belonging to its Sunni adherents. And it declares war on Western nations. This presents a hybrid seldom seen before. Unlike al-Qaeda or a criminal syndicate, the Islamic State declares war under the banners of war. Because, for the time being at least, the United States is carrying out its war against the Islamic State from the air, it may not confront the problem of whether to send captured members of IS to interminable prison terms in Guantanamo. But, presuming allied Arab armies designated to carry out ground operations capture IS fighters, they will make up their own rules as to their treatment and they quite possibly will not be according to the Marquess of Queensberry rules.

The point to be made out of all this has to do with the rise of a form of conflict not seen since the emergence of nation-states in the mid–seventeenth century. In the age of the nation-state, the license to commit violence was held by the state exclusively. In one of life's great ironies, the legalization of warfare by nation-states led civilized nations to negotiate conditions under which warfare would be conducted. These became the Geneva Conventions. Violation of these conventions would lead, as they did for much of the German high command following World War II, to trials for war crimes, that is to say, for conducting war without following the rules.

In the twenty-first century, violence now operates outside any organized structures and certainly outside the constraints of international laws of warfare. It has reverted to the pre–nation-state era of barbarism and is purely criminal in nature.

To complicate this confusion, some states harbor groups committed to terrorist tactics, and other states, especially in the Middle East, finance directly or indirectly the operations of those groups. Thus, the United States may cultivate friendly relations with a country that is helping to finance groups intent on killing Americans. Given the intricate movements of money internationally, it is often difficult if not impossible to track this financing. Nevertheless, intelligence agencies are sure that it is happening if for no other reason than the contributing nation is buying protection from terrorists by paying blackmail.

Dealing with disorganized violence in years to come will require the skills of both the military and the police. But regardless of the skills required, the culprits will continue to have more in common with criminals than with warriors. It will not be surprising if continued efforts to suppress terrorist cells produce a hybrid quasi-military force that combines crime prevention with small-unit special military forces. Recent transfer of surplus military hardware to local police forces has already taken us a major step in that direction.

The major issue, however, is less the force used to combat terrorism than the set of laws and institutions employed to impose justice upon it. Vague categories such as "enemy combatants" and obscure facilities such as Guantanamo Bay are not the answer.

THE EXPEDITIONARY STATE

The Cold War and the war on terror that followed led the United States to engage in foreign expeditions large and small that departed from the admonition of our nation's founders to avoid foreign entanglements.

In the fall of 2014, we went to war against the Islamic State in Iraq and Syria. We did so because the Islamic State was threatening to overrun Baghdad and thus take over a nation we invaded in 2003 in a badly mistaken effort to find al-Qaeda. As al-Qaeda made the Taliban in Afghanistan look relatively ineffective, so the Islamic State is so violently extremist as to be disowned by al-Qaeda. As we were to learn in Afghanistan and Iraq, and even in Vietnam before then, waging war against insurgencies is a fundamentally different enterprise than waging war against a country such as Germany or Japan. The enemy is fluid, has no capital, and can melt into the countryside. And, having engaged in two recent prolonged wars, the Obama administration limited its war on the Islamic State to air power alone, supposing (mostly hoping) that indigenous Muslim armies in the region would carry out the land combat. The goal of "debilitating and destroying" the Islamic State cannot be achieved in this way in less than two or three decades, according to senior military commanders.

So this third prolonged war in the Middle East is only the latest in a long series of foreign engagements by the United States following World War II. Those Obama critics in Congress repeatedly calling for him to "do something" in Syria now find themselves required to support this obscure, and potentially impossible, mission. But they will resume their opposition to the operation when it almost inevitably does not quickly succeed. The lesson is this: Armed conflict in the twenty-first century will not yield itself to quick and final results.

The first major U.S. military engagement of this type was in Korea in 1950 as the leader of the United Nations authorized operations to prevent the North Korean army, backed by the People's Republic of China, from overrunning South Korea. The Korean War lasted three years and produced almost fifty thousand casualties.

Slightly more than a decade later, South Vietnam was faced with increasing incursions from North Vietnam and our commitment of military advisors eventually led to the deployment of more than a half-million U.S. military personnel before

North Vietnamese forces overran the South. Unlike in Korea, a massive U.S. military engagement failed to prevent the collapse of our ally.

Thereafter, the United States invaded Panama to oust its president, Manuel Noriega, and prevent what was perceived to be the nationalization of the Panama Canal. We invaded the tiny Caribbean island of Grenada in 1983 for reasons still unclear but ostensibly to rescue medical students.

Saddam Hussein's invasion of Kuwait in 1990 threatened world oil supplies and offered a precedent for territorially hungry oligarchs everywhere. Encouraged by Prime Minister Margaret Thatcher, President George H. W. Bush declared, "This will not stand." Mrs. Thatcher, as many allies did over the years, had in mind that U.S. military forces would lead the charge. The commander of U.S. forces, General Colin Powell, uttered a memorable declaration for the late twentieth century: "If you break it, you own it." By the time the first President Bush's son invaded Iraq again a decade later, this admonition was brushed aside and we are still being called upon to redeploy forces to salvage a badly broken Iraq.

After considerable delay, the United States bombed Serbia in 1999 to prevent further ethnic bloodshed in Kosovo. Then came 9/11 and the war on terror. And an initial operation by U.S. Special Forces to neutralize Osama bin Laden and the Taliban that had sheltered him soon gave way to all-out war in Afghanistan. That operation was prolonged by the shift of focus to the invasion of Iraq, which resulted in a prolonged decade-long war in both nations.

Not all venues of conflict drew the United States' military attention. The slaughter of 800,000 Tutsis in Rwanda was left to run its course, as were other regional and tribal conflicts. But, despite notable setbacks such as the failed "Black Hawk Down" raid in Mogadishu, by and large the United States foreign policy during the second half of the twentieth century and the first decade of the twenty-first was one characterized by military intervention, in some cases for prolonged periods of time and with high casualty rates.

United States policy makers have not been particularly astute at calculating the consequences of foreign expeditions. To put it bluntly—invasions have consequences, consequences few politicians wish to contemplate when their blood runs hot. The most recent case in point is Gulf War I. Preparing to repel Iraq's invasion of Kuwait required a substantial military buildup that took months to achieve. U.S. headquarters for this operation was located in Saudi Arabia, considered throughout the Muslim world as the locale of its holiest sites. The birth of al-Qaeda, according to virtually all sources that have documented its rise, can be traced to this "Crusader" occupation of the country where these holy sites are located. The degree to which the long-term implications of this massive military operation in Saudi Arabia figured in the first Bush administration's calculations has never been made clear.

If warnings of these implications were raised in invasion planning by senior officials, no one has stepped forward to document them.

Once again, the lack of understanding of foreign histories and cultures in the use of U.S. military force in an expeditionary capacity came back to haunt us, in this case with the attacks of 9/11 that caused a fundamental alteration of our domestic lives, the rise of the homeland security state, a war on terror, and a dramatic increase in intelligence intrusiveness at home and abroad.

The Vietnam War marked the reversal of political party roles. Throughout much of the twentieth century, Democratic administrations under presidents Wilson, Roosevelt, Truman, Kennedy, and Johnson caused their party to be seen as the war party, and throughout much of that period, Republicans were reluctant to send troops abroad and incur the costs and complications such deployments inevitably incurred.

Following Vietnam, however, Democrats became the antiwar party and Republicans took the lead in advocating the use of military force. Despite the traditional argument of Republican vice presidential candidate Robert Dole in the 1976 campaign that Democrats "get us into war," his party was rapidly transforming itself into the war party.

For our purposes, the issue is less about partisan politics and more about America's role in the world of the twenty-first century and whether and how that role should comport with the strongly held belief of our nation's founders that our country should not, in Secretary of State John Quincy Adams's words, "go abroad seeking demons to destroy."

For strategic purposes, the United States is an island nation with broad oceans on its eastern and western coasts and friendly neighbors to the north and south. Our founders were schooled in seemingly endless European wars, the Hundred Years' War, the War of the Roses, Napoleonic excursions, British-French conflicts, wars for territory and religious wars, shifting alliances, diplomatic duplicity, and wars for resources. Despite this, the founders sometimes were divided over whether to ally with England or France.

The predominant view in American foreign policy circles since the end of World War II has been that we had no choice but to be engaged in the world; that Communism was on the march, especially in the postcolonial Third World; that withdrawal from Europe and Asia would invite a political vacuum potentially filled by fascist, imperialist, and Communist aggression that would result in the remobilization of the United States for the third time in the twentieth century.

Thus, contrary to almost 165 years of American history, we found ourselves the sole superpower, the single greatest force for security and stability in the world. Filling that role required the maintenance and gradual expansion of a vast network of military bases, outposts, and naval ports throughout the world, especially in postwar Europe and Asia. That role further required us to intervene when allies were threatened, as in South Korea, or when local ethnic conflict, as in Serbia and Kosovo, threatened regional stability.

But the realities of the first quarter of the twenty-first century are significantly different from the realities of the previous century. International markets are integrated by globalization and are interdependent. We borrow huge amounts of Chinese money to finance our deficits and buy its goods. Most democratic nations are happy to let the United States tax its citizens to police the world and enforce security and stability.

Alas, we do not live in an age of peace and tranquility. With the collapse of Communist ideology as an aggressive alternative to democracy, more traditional belief systems returned to demand loyalty. The rise of ethnic nationalism, religious fundamentalism, and tribes, clans, and gangs marked the fragmentation of nation-states and the disintegration of national loyalties. National economies blurred into international financial and commercial networks. New communications technologies destroyed autocratic nations' monopoly on information.

The nation-state found it increasingly difficult to guarantee its citizens' security through its traditional monopoly on violence. Into this vacuum came stateless nations armed to the teeth from black-market arsenals scattered throughout the world. Faced with insecurity, ethnic groups and tribes took up arms to fill the security vacuum and demanded loyalty in exchange for protection. For elites, a fantastic growth in private security operations occurred worldwide. The very nature of conflict experienced a transformation from traditional warfare to unconventional, irregular warfare carried out by dispersed networks of militia.

Beginning in Vietnam, if not before, highly trained, heavily equipped, and large-unit U.S. land forces, augmented by superior air cover, bombing missions, and offshore artillery fire, found themselves searching for small units that melted into jungles and refused to participate in traditional set-piece battles. The new warriors refused to play fair. Those who did not learn the lessons of Vietnam were doomed to learn them in Afghanistan and Iraq.

The dramatic end of the Cold War, basically in a seventy-two-hour period at the end of August 1991, provided a historic opportunity to reshape our military forces for the coming new century. Alas, we did not take it. Instead, successive administrations, presidents, and secretaries of defense perpetuated big army divisions, nuclear aircraft-carrier task groups, and long-range bomber wings. All this cost fortunes that might have been better spent elsewhere, including in maintaining and rebuilding the nation's public infrastructure necessary for economic growth.

One lingering question is whether we have learned anything from America's history of assassinations. It is unfortunate that senior administration officials making life-and-death decisions today on when, where, and against whom drone strikes should be launched did not live through, as I did, the period of 1975–76 when congressional investigations, including the Church Committee's, discovered plots by our government to assassinate foreign leaders. In the case of Fidel Castro, those plots had an almost demented insistence and caused the CIA to partner with the Mafia to achieve the objectives that were ordered by at least two administrations.

Profound Constitutional and moral issues were raised by these plots and their discoveries. For a new and very young senator, it was shocking to discover that a sewer of still-unknown dimensions was flowing underneath the city on a hill. Such a discovery causes you to suspect almost everyone and everything and to believe that expediency will trump principle on almost every occasion.

The drone-assassination policy is the product of the confluence of the notion of preemption; terrorism as war, not crime; and a mistaken notion that "national security" can be defined so broadly that any action is justified. At least one prominent Air Force general desperately wanted to initiate large-scale nuclear attacks on the Soviet Union in the 1940s. Presumably, the preemptive doctrine would have justified massive bombing raids on the imperial palace and Japanese Ministry of War if we had known they were planning Pearl Harbor. These actions are possible if you put aside what the United States of America claims to stand for.

We should not be willing to trust unnamed "informed, high-level officials" with unchecked and unbalanced assassination decisions. Information is often wrong, and who knows how high "high" is? Who puts the hit list together using what information? Both parties have their Ollie Norths (originators of bizarre international schemes that confuse our friends and bewilder fellow Americans). Ronald Reagan signed a paper authorizing Iran-Contra but couldn't remember doing so. And what are the standards for determining an "imminent threat of violent attacks"? These are vague and subjective standards and there is no congressional oversight or judicial review.

Where American citizens are targeted, as they have been, their Constitutional rights are unilaterally suspended by the anonymous "high-level official." That is not what Madison or Jefferson had in mind. Having drones available would not have altered their principles, as they seem to have done with those in power today. And, politically, Democrats have to be very careful on this issue to avoid adoption of a double standard. All hell would break loose among Democrats if drone assassinations had been carried out by the George W. Bush administration.

Expediency is never a justification for unconstitutional and immoral actions. This is so even where self-defense and national security are concerned. It has proved incredibly easy to assassinate someone (and his family) half a world away. And that is what makes this new style of warfare so attractive—and so dangerous. The Obama administration is creating precedents it will live to regret and inviting retaliation that uses both drones and computers as they become available to most nations in the world.

We believe ourselves to be exceptional, and when we live up to our Constitutional principles, we are. But when we abandon those principles simply because new technology makes it easy to do so, we become just like everyone else, lose our moral authority, and welcome our behavior to be used against us.

All of which leads to the question of America's role in the twenty-first century and how much of that role will continue to be based on military power even though on a smaller scale. Barack Obama is the first American president to confront these issues on a daily basis. The Ukrainian-Russian conflict tests both our willingness and our capability to support a non-NATO nation in conflict with its much larger and more powerful neighbor.

Our outrage at the Russian annexation of the Crimea, traditionally a Russian possession, neglected to consider our role in forcing the secession of Kosovo in 2008 after the Serbian crisis. Though the circumstances differ, it is a caution against double standards and hypocrisy in foreign conduct. The same is true of our even greater outrage over the probable use of Russian missiles in shooting down Malaysia Airlines Flight 17 over eastern Ukraine. The U.S. Navy mistakenly shot down

Iran Air Flight 655 in Iranian air space in 1988 with 290 killed.

The prolonged Syrian civil war confronts us with the question of whether and how to support insurgents operating in league with religious fundamentalists. Intervention in Syria became even more problematic in recent months with the rise of the self-proclaimed Islamic State.

The Israeli-Palestinian conflict, seemingly irresolvable, presents the conundrum of supporting a trusted ally while seeking to limit the damage it does to civilian populations. We need China to invest in our bonds even as we try to offset its maritime ambitions in the East and South China Seas. We are negotiating an end to Iran's nuclear ambitions as much as anything to preempt Israeli air strikes that could ignite a major regional war.

The Obama dilemma results from assuming office after two expensive and unresolved wars that caused citizen exhaustion and confusion over the fact that these wars did not lend themselves to "victory" in any traditional sense. And, even as large majorities of Americans wanted rapid liquidation of these ventures, both liberal and neoconservative interventionists clamored for American "action" and "leadership," usually undefined, in response to these and other global conflicts. When forced to define action and leadership, both factions usually confess to wanting military force to be employed.

United States foreign and military policy in the second half of the twentieth century and the early part of this century is characterized by ignorance of the situations in which we intervened. Just as we mistook Vietnamese nationalist ambitions for ideological ones, we also did not fully appreciate the 1,400 years of Sunni-Shia conflict that has defined and divided the Muslim world and how the invasion of two Muslim countries might unleash these dormant and violent forces from Afghanistan to Lebanon. Our experiences in Vietnam, Afghanistan, and Iraq offer lessons in understanding national, religious, and cultural histories before blundering into conflicts we know little about. Whether these lessons have been fully learned is yet to be determined.

There is a deeper lesson, though, for U.S. policy makers and presumed foreign policy elites. That lesson has to do with our motivations for intervention. Currently, there are four dominant schools of thought: liberal interventionists motivated by human rights concerns; neoconservative interventionists motivated by national security and power-projection interests; foreign policy realists motivated by acceptance of the world as it is and recognition of other nations' interests; and libertarians motivated by concerns for the limits of American power and the financial costs involved in long-term military deployments and entanglements.

The libertarian neo-isolationist school of thought at least recognizes the limits of American understanding of foreign histories and cultures, and responds by advocating that we just stay home. For both liberal and neoconservative interventionists, however, an understanding of context is secondary to intense feelings about human rights or power projection. An aspect of the Obama dilemma is his apparent concern for historical context under circumstances where information is murky at best and nonexistent at worst. Our history is so characterized by "shoot first and ask questions later" that we have yet to develop the mature, sophisticated understanding of foreign cultures and histories necessary to devise wise policies.

Even in our third century of existence, statecraft is in short supply in America. Instead, we have substituted "intelligence" for statecraft. The assumption behind the expenditure of $40 billion or more annually on the so-called intelligence community is that quantity is an acceptable alternative to quality. The more information we collect, the smarter we will be. That theory has not served us well. Our ability to vacuum up vast quantities of data has far outrun our ability to know what it means.

Statesmanship is rare. It requires experience in foreign venues and acquaintance with foreign leaders. Even more, it requires a sophisticated sense of human motivation, a knowledge of foreign cultures and their history, an understanding of the interests of others, and a perspective on what is and is not important. Keen judgment, above all, is required. Few genuine statesmen are ideologues, partisans, or hard-liners of one kind or another. Statesmanship requires objectivity and a degree of detachment from the passions of the day. Perspective is difficult to achieve if one is swept up in heated argument.

If we choose to remain an expeditionary state, statesmanship must replace ideology and political demagoguery. We will have to insist on much greater knowledge of the culture we are parachuting into and the probable costs and consequences we are creating.

THE SURVEILLANCE STATE

From the time the Church Committee was impaneled in 1975 until today, the so-called intelligence community has become a giant intelligence metropolis. Not only have the number and sizes of the U.S. government agencies exploded, but they are now augmented by a bizarre network of private consulting companies, one of which employed Mr. Snowden. It is not clear whether even the president of the United States knows how many people and how many tax dollars are involved in this.

Much of this postdates the terrorist attacks of September 11, 2001. The United States now has deployed a greater array of intelligence-collection operations against free-range terrorist groups than it did against the Soviet Union and the entire Communist Bloc. And the dangers for civil liberties and the Constitutional rights of Americans are much greater. Whether months or years from now, we will learn of the breadth and depth of the abuse of power in our Constitutional democracy. The facts will come out. It is only a matter of time.

As with Watergate and CIA excesses such as assassination plots, the question is why massive wrongdoing can take place for so long without it being discovered. We give special Constitutional protection to a free press so that serious abuses of power will be disclosed. This is a much more legitimate function of a free press than the relatively recent window peeking in search of personal "scandals." Since the passage of the National Security Act of 1947, however, every administration, none more so than the incumbent Obama administration, has used the national security argument, often illegitimately, to prevent even those diminished elements of the media genuinely concerned with unconstitutional abuses of power from telling the American public what national security is costing them in terms of rights and freedoms.

Where all this stops is anyone's guess. There are always new, and highly expensive, technologies to try out. Overhead satellites can see objects smaller than a basketball from a hundred miles up. Tiny drones can take pictures in private windows. Conversations can be recorded from blocks away. The list of capabilities is virtually endless. And it all follows the iron law of security and technology: If it can be done, it will be done. In the intelligence world, self-restraint is not a virtue.

It is self-evident that our founders did not know nor could they have anticipated where twenty-first-century technology would take us in information collection, including from our own citizens. They did, however, create a government of checks and balances, including Constitutional requirements for Congress, the representatives of the people, to oversee the activities of the executive branch, including its now massive intelligence networks. This requirement was not being attended to until Church Committee recommendations led to the creation of intelligence oversight committees as recently as 1977. Between the creation of the CIA in 1947 and then, Congress simply did not want to know and did not want to do its job in this murky arena.

"We must guard against the acquisition of unwarranted influence, whether sought or unsought, by the military-industrial complex. The potential for the disastrous rise of misplaced power exists, and will persist." Thus spoke President Dwight Eisenhower in January 1961.

Now we have an intelligence-industrial complex composed of close to a dozen and a half federal intelligence agencies and services, many of which are duplicative, that are supported by a growing private-sector intelligence world. Originally initiated in the National Security Act of 1947 as instrumental in conducting the Cold War, this massive expansion of data collection and analysis continued on even after the Cold War ended in 1991 and then received renewed energy with the declaration of a "global war on terrorism."

Following the discovery by the Church Committee of serious unconstitutional abuses of power in the early 1970s, steps were taken to protect Constitutional rights, especially Fourth Amendment protections against unreasonable searches and seizures, most notably by the creation of Foreign Intelligence Surveillance Act (FISA) courts, which were required to issue warrants for surveillance, as the Fourth Amendment requires, upon a showing that the national security is endangered.

But even this protection, as important as it is, seems less than adequate when the record shows that virtually all government requests for warrants for surveillance are granted by these courts. Even if a new layer of Constitutional ombudsman who could appear in the secret FISA court to question the government's case was added, serious questions of privacy and personal security and the explosion of the intelligence-industrial complex would remain.

As we ponder the motivations and personalities of the Snowdens and the Assanges, we must not lose sight of the greatest question: Is the Surveillance State—the intelligence-industrial complex—out of the control of the elected officials responsible for holding it accountable to American citizens protected by the U.S. Constitution? We should not have to rely on whistle-blowers to protect our rights.

Someone or some ones must be empowered by the White House and Congress to take an Olympian view of the intelligence-industrial complex, to downsize it, reorganize it, provide strict rules for its conduct and operations, and eliminate the metastasizing private consulting world now overwhelming it. In 2004 Congress created the position of Director of National Intelligence to do something like this. It has not worked.

The case of Edward Snowden, and future Snowdens, will continue to draw great media attention. But, while we are preoccupied by the character of the renegade, the larger historical question remains: How do we stop the growth of the intelligence-industrial complex? Intelligence is no longer a restrained, focused security function of a nation engaged in a Cold War. It is an industry and a huge one at that. Ships, planes, tanks, and missiles are immense burdens on our treasury. Information collection is an even more consequential burden on our democracy, our freedom, and our rights.

Presidents and members of Congress err on the side of security. No elected official wants a terrorist attack on an American city on his or her watch. Better to err on the side of intrusiveness than to risk loss of lives. A majority of Americans undoubtedly approve of that erring stance. But we must always weigh in the bargain the cost to our democracy and the loss of our rights.

The slogan during the Cold War was "Better dead than Red." Today the slogan is "Better alive in Big Brother's state than risk the next Twin Towers." When confronted with this new reality, I cannot help but think of the statement the director of the U.S. Secret Service said to me and my wife when I became a candidate for president. "If someone wants to kill you," he said, "he will probably kill you. Our job is to make it as difficult as possible."

In the age of terrorism, that is roughly the place we are in as Americans. There is no absolute security. We are trading part of our freedom for the hope of staying alive, of making the next bin Laden's job as difficult as possible. The question we must ask ourselves is this: At what point does the loss of liberty outweigh the risk of life itself?

It is the question most penetratingly raised by Fyodor Dostoyevsky in *The Brothers Karamazov.* In the bargain offered by the Grand Inquisitor, the choice was bread or freedom. In exchange for bread, his institution, church or state, required the sacrifice of freedom. Today his bread would be security. Give me your freedom, and I will provide security. We have yet to reach this ultimate point but we are well down the road toward it.

This is the bargain always offered by authoritarian and totalitarian states for millennia. It is a bargain Americans have never had to face, even during the Cold War, until now. We are not at, perhaps not even near, the point of no return, but we need prophets to warn us of the dangers ahead and force us to consider our values.

THE SPECIAL INTEREST STATE

As noted at the outset, four qualities have distinguished republican government from ancient Athens forward: the sovereignty of the people; a sense of the common good; government dedicated to the commonwealth; and resistance to corruption. Measured against the standards established for republics from ancient times, the American Republic is massively corrupt.

From Plato and Aristotle forward, corruption was meant to describe actions and decisions that put a narrow, special, or personal interest ahead of the interest of the public or commonwealth. Corruption did not have to stoop to money under the table, vote buying, or even renting out the Lincoln bedroom. In the governing of a republic, corruption was self-interest placed above the interest of all—the public interest.

By that standard, can anyone seriously doubt that our republic, our government, is corrupt? There have been Teapot Domes and financial scandals of one kind or another throughout our nation's history. There has never been a time, however, when the government of the United States was so perversely and systematically dedicated to special interests, earmarks, side deals, log-rolling, vote-trading, and sweetheart deals of one kind or another.

What brought us to this? We were brought to this by a sinister system combining staggering campaign costs, political contributions, political action committees, special interest payments for access, and, most of all, the rise of the lobbying class.

Worst of all, the army of lobbyists that started relatively small in the mid-twentieth century has now grown to big battalions of law firms and lobbying firms of the right, left, and an amalgam of both. And that gargantuan, if not reptilian, industry now takes on board former members of the House and the Senate and their personal and committee staffs. And they are all getting fabulously rich.

This development in recent years has been so insidious that it now goes without notice. The key word is not quid-pro-quo bribery, the key word is *access*. In exchange for a few moments of the senator's time and many more moments of her committee staff's time, fund-raising events with the promise of tens, even hundreds, of thousands of dollars are delivered.

Corruption in a federated republic such as ours operates vertically as well as horizontally. Seeing how business is conducted in Washington, it did not take long for governors of both parties across the country to subscribe to the special interest state. Both the Republican and Democratic governors' associations formed "social welfare" organizations composed of wealthy interests and corporate executives to raise money for their respective parties in exchange for close, personal access to individual governors, governors who almost surely could render executive decisions favorable to those corporate interests. A series of judicial decisions enabled these "social welfare" groups, supposedly barred from political activity, to channel virtually unlimited amounts of money to governors in exchange for access, the political coin of the realm in the corrupted republic, and to do so out of sight of the American people. Editorially, the *New York Times* commented that "the stealthy form of political corruption known as 'dark money' now fully permeates governor's offices around the country, allowing corporations to push past legal barriers and gather enormous influence."

Frustrated, irate discussions of this legalized corruption are met in the Washington media with a shrug. So what? Didn't we just have dinner with that lobbyist for the banking industry, or the teachers' union, or the airline industry at that well-known journalist's house only two nights ago? Fine lady, and she used to be the chairman of one of those powerful committees. I gather she is using her Rolodex rather skillfully on behalf of her new clients. Illegal? Not at all. Just smart . . . and so charming.

There is little wonder that Americans of the right and the

left and many in the middle are apoplectic at their government and absolutely, and rightly, convinced that the game of government is rigged in favor of the elite and the powerful. Occupiers see even more wealth rising to the top at the expense of the poor and the middle class. And Tea Partiers believe their tax dollars are going to well-organized welfare parasites and government bureaucrats.

Recent months have seen, in effect, the legalization of Watergate. Who would have thought, forty years after the greatest political scandal and presidential abuse of power in U.S. history, that the Supreme Court of the United States would rule the practices that financed that scandal were now legal?

That is essentially the effect of the *Citizens United* decision. Bets may be taken as to the length of time that will expire before this tsunami of political money ends up in the pockets of break-in burglars, wiretap experts, surveillance magicians, and cyberpunks. Given the power and money at stake in presidential and congressional elections, it is inevitable that candidates or their operatives with larceny in their hearts will tap into the hundreds of millions of dollars that their campaigns are awash in to game the system in highly illegal ways.

And, of course, the ultimate victims of the corruption of the democratic process are not defeated candidates and parties but America's citizens. Perhaps Supreme Court justices should have to experience a corrupted election process firsthand to recognize a hollowed-out democracy. As one who experienced Watergate in its multi-tentacled form, I know it is not pleasant to be placed under surveillance, to have your taxes audited, and to experience dirty tricks. All this happened to me, among a number of others, simply because we worked for an honest presidential candidate who dared challenge the authority and power of a president who had long since forgotten the integrity the democratic process requires.

The advent of legalized corruption launched by the Supreme Court empowers the superrich to fund their own presidential and congressional campaigns as pet projects, to foster pet policies, and to represent pet political enclaves. You have a billion, or even several hundred million, then purchase a candidate from the endless reserve bench of minor politicians and make him or her a star, a mouthpiece for any cause or purpose however questionable, and that candidate will mouth your script in endless political debates and through as many television spots as you are willing to pay for. All legal now.

To compound the political felony, much, if not most, campaign financing is now carried out in secret, so that everyday citizens have a decreasing ability to determine to whom their elected officials are beholden and to whom they must now give special access. As recently as the 2014 election, the facts documented this government of influence by secrecy: "More than half of the general election advertising aired by outside groups in the battle for control of Congress," according to the *New York Times*, "has come from organizations that disclose little or nothing about their donors, a flood of secret money that is now at the center of a debate over the line between free speech and corruption."

The five prevailing Supreme Court justices, holding that a legal entity called a corporation has First Amendment rights of free speech, might at least have required the bought-and-paid-for candidates to wear sponsor labels on their suits as stock-car drivers do. Though, for the time being, sponsored candidates will not be openly promoted by Exxon-Mobil or the Stardust Resort and Casino but by phony "committees for good government" smokescreens.

To add to the profound misdirection of American politics by the Supreme Court, we now have what might be called convergence in the garden of government influence.

Back in the 1960s Flannery O'Connor wrote the short story "Everything That Rises Must Converge." It had to do with generational insensitivity between a mother and son, and between generations on the issue of race in society. In reading a piece by Thomas B. Edsall ("The Lobbyist in the Gray Flannel Suit," *New York Times*, May 14, 2012), this title came to mind in a totally different context. The context is the lobbying maze in Washington and the convergence of dozens of noxious weeds in the garden of government into a handful of giant predator thornbushes now devouring that garden.

Of this handful, the largest by far is WPP (originally called Wire and Plastic Products; is there a metaphor here?), which has its headquarters in London and more than 150,000 employees in 2,500 offices spread around 107 countries. It, together with one or two conglomerating competitors, represents a fourth branch of government, vacuuming up former senators and House members and their spouses and families, key committee staff, former senior administration officials of both parties and several administrations, and ambassadors, diplomats, and retired senior military officers.

WPP has swallowed giant public relations, advertising, and lobbying outfits such as Hill & Knowlton and Burson-Marsteller, along with dozens of smaller members of the highly lucrative special interest and influence-manipulation world. Close behind WPP is the Orwellian-named Omnicom Group and another converger vaguely called the Interpublic Group of Companies. According to Mr. Edsall, WPP had billings last year of $72.3 billion, larger than the budgets of quite a number of countries.

With a budget so astronomical, think how much good WPP can do in the campaign finance arena, especially since the *Citizens United* decision. The possibilities are almost limitless. Why pay for a senator or congresswoman here or there when you can buy an entire committee? Think of the banks that can be bailed out, the range of elaborate weapons systems that can be sold to the government, the protection from congressional scrutiny that can be paid for, the economic policies that can be manipulated.

The lobbying business is no longer about votes up or down on particular measures that may emerge in Congress or policies made in the White House. It is about setting agendas, deciding what should and should not be brought up for hearings and legislation. We have gone way beyond mere vote buying now. The converging Influence World represents nothing less than an unofficial but enormously powerful fourth branch of government.

To whom is this branch of government accountable? Who sets the agenda for its rising army of influence marketers? How easy will it be to not only go from office to a lucrative lobbying job but, more important, from lucrative lobbying job to holding office? Where are its loyalties if it is manipulating and influencing governments around the world? Other than as a trough of money of gigantic proportions, how does it view the government of the United States?

America's founders knew one thing: The republics of history all died when narrow interests overwhelmed the common good and the interests of the commonwealth.

O'Connor took her story title from a belief of the French Jesuit philosopher Pierre Teilhard de Chardin. Teilhard de Chardin believed that all good would rise and that all that rose would eventually converge. We pray that he was right for, at the present moment, we have only prayer and no evidence. In the realm of twenty-first-century American politics, the opposite is surely coming true.

Welcome to the Age of Vanity politics and campaigns-for-hire featuring candidates who repeat their sponsored messages like ice-cream-truck vendors passing through the neighborhood. If the current Supreme Court had been sitting during Watergate in 1974, it would not have voted 9–0 to require the president to turn over legally incriminating tapes but instead would have voted to support the use of illegal campaign contributions to finance criminal cover-ups as an exercise in "free speech."

What would our founders make of this nightmare of corruption? We only know, in Thomas Jefferson's case, for example, that his distrust of central government had to do with the well-founded and prescient suspicion that its largesse would go to powerful and influential interests, especially financiers, who knew how to manipulate both the government and the financial markets. In particular, Jefferson envisioned sophisticated bankers speculating in public-debt issues with some if not all the interest incurred going into their pockets.

He was way ahead of his time. The limits of his imagination would not have encompassed the early twenty-first-century financial world where vast sums of money are manipulated like the world's greatest three-card-monte game and nothing tangible is being produced—except fees and more money. Even the titans ruling over this game confessed, after the 2008 financial collapse, that they did not know what collateralized debt obligations, bundled derivatives, and other tricky instruments devised by clever twenty-eight-year-olds were about. All they knew was how to respond to their industry lobbyists' requests for very large contributions to compliant members of congressional finance committees and to do so quickly and often. And they did get their money's worth.

The scope and scale of this genuine scandal (as distinguished from vastly more mundane behavior that passes for scandal in the media) is the single greatest threat to our form of government. It is absolutely incompatible with the principles and ideals upon which America was founded. At the very least, we Americans cannot hold ourselves up to the world as the beacon of democracy so long as we permit, as long as we acquiesce in, corruption so far beyond the standards of the true republic that our government cannot be proclaimed an ideal for other aspiring nations.

On a more personal level, how can public service be promoted as an ideal to young people when this sewer corrupts our Republic? At this point in early twenty-first-century America, the greatest service our nation's young people could provide is to lead an army of outraged young Americans armed with brooms on a crusade to sweep out the rascals and rid our capital of the money changers, rent seekers, revolving-door dancers, and special interest deal makers and power brokers and send them back home to make an honest living, that is, if they still remember how to do so.

What angers truly patriotic Americans is that this entire

Augean stable is legal. Even worse, recent Supreme Court decisions placing corporations under the First Amendment protection of free speech for political purposes compounds the tragedy of American democracy. For all practical political purposes, the government of the United States is for sale to the highest bidder.

A harsh judgment? Indeed. But it is impossible to claim to love one's country and not be outraged at how corrupt it has become. For former senators and representatives to trade a title given them by the voters of their respective states and districts for cash is beyond shameful. It is outrageous.

"I tremble for my country when I contemplate that God is just." Those words of Thomas Jefferson, enshrined on the walls of his memorial, referred to the institution of slavery. Today he might readily render the same judgment about corruption in and of the American Republic.

Imagine if you will the response of George Washington, James Madison, Jefferson, John Adams, and even the financial pragmatist Alexander Hamilton were they to observe today's lobbyists at work, especially former government officials, organizing fund-raising events and delivering bundles of checks. They would be appalled. Even more, they would be ashamed.

Can this bazaar of special interest stalls in the halls of Congress, the money changers in the temple of democracy, be justified by the realities of modern times? If so, it is not readily apparent how. America can be a mass democracy of 330 million people. It is engaged commercially, diplomatically, and militarily all over the world. We live in an age of instant communication and international travel. The amounts of money involved in administering our government are staggering, with appreciably more zeros than even in the 1970s and '80s. But none of these facts lift the burden of ethics in public life, what the founders called virtue, from the shoulders of public servants.

It is an error of serious proportion to dismiss corruption in twenty-first-century American democracy on the grounds that this has all been going on from the beginning, that boys will be boys, that politicians are always on the take. Past incidents of the violation of public ethics provide no argument for accepting the systemic and cancerous commercialization of modern American politics.

For that is what it is. Political office, public service, and engagement in governance must not be monetized. Even if no laws are broken, even if a public servant can walk out the door one day and cash in his or her experience and title for cash the next, *that does not make it right*. Everything strictly legal is not therefore ethical. When the founders discussed virtue, they were harking back to ancient Athens and the ideal of the republic. And, as scholars of ancient Greek and Roman political texts, they knew in their minds and in their hearts that a republic with leaders who lacked virtue would not long survive.

That is the issue. With the dubious endorsement by the Supreme Court of the United States, which will have its own history to answer to, using First Amendment protection of free speech to legitimize the most egregious violations of the principles of the republic is to invite the eventual erosion of the ideal of the American Republic, to reduce this great nation and its heritage to the worst kind of mundane governance, to prostitute a noble experiment on the altar of expediency and greed, and to leave coming generations to ponder what went wrong.

"Just because it is legal doesn't make it right" should be carved above every congressional doorway, every cabinet department, and even the White House itself. Contrast the fact that upon returning to Independence, Missouri, in 1953, Harry Truman refused to take even a pencil from the White House ("It didn't belong to me," he said, by way of explanation) with modern presidents whose political networks have graciously waited until they departed the White House to make them rich.

Though quaintly used in recent times to denote proper behavior for ladies, virtue as applied to public service is a powerful standard. It genuinely does require having no personal interest in the public's business, not only at the time one is involved in decision making but also thereafter. The fact that many former presidents and prime ministers of European democracies have enriched themselves in questionable ways after leaving office does not justify similar behavior on the part of American politicians. We hold ourselves to a higher standard.

Our ancestors did not depart Europe and elsewhere to seek freedom and self-government alone. They came to these shores to escape social and political systems that were corrosive and corrupt. Two and a quarter centuries later, we are returning to those European practices. We are in danger of becoming a different kind of nation, one our founders would not recognize and would deplore.

Even as politicians and pundits alike pummel the fiscal deficit, we are developing an integrity deficit of mounting proportions. And one is not disconnected from the other. Because of the erosion of the integrity of our governing system, and the principles and ideals underlying it, the fiscal deficit increases. The government spending so many conservatives claim to abhor includes not only the social safety net of Roosevelt and Johnson, but also the war-making excursions of Ronald Reagan and George W. Bush. It is all government spending. And it includes favorite pork-barrel projects of every member of both houses of Congress of both political parties, and every one of those most loudly condemning "wasteful government spending." Those projects are produced by the lobbying interests that raise money for those members of Congress in direct proportion to their effectiveness at bringing government-financed projects to their states and districts. By definition, if it is a project in my state or district, it is not wasteful.

Restoration of the Republic of Conscience requires reduction and eventual elimination of the integrity deficit. Virtue, the disinterestedness of our elected officials, must replace political careerism and special interests. The national interest, what is best for our country and coming generations, must replace struggles for power, bitter partisanship, and ideological rigidity. This is not dreamy idealism; it is an idealism rooted in the original purpose of this nation.

We were not created to be like other nations. We were created as an alternative to monarchy, aristocracy, oligarchy, and corrupt political systems. The more we follow the easy path, the one paved for the benefit of the wealthy and powerful, the more we stray from our originally intended purpose and the more we lose our unique purpose for existence.

Will America continue to offer a comfortable life for many? I hope so. Will we continue to have a strong army? If we are willing to pay for it, yes. Will we continue to provide the world's entertainment? I presume so. But these are not the real questions.

The question is: By adhering to its highest principles and ideals, will America continue to have the moral authority to lead all people of goodwill? The answer remains to be seen. And that answer will have much to do with whether we have the courage to drive the money changers from the temple of democracy and recapture government of the people, for the people, and by the people.

In addition to the rise of the national security state, and the concentration of wealth and power in America, no development in modern times sets us apart more from the nation originally bequeathed to us than the rise of the special interest state. There is a Gresham's law related to the republican ideal. Bad politics drives out good politics. Legalized corruption drives men and women of stature, honor, and dignity out of the halls of government. Self-respecting individuals cannot long tolerate a system of election and reelection so dependent on cultivating the favor of those known to expect access in return. Such a system is corrosive to the soul.

Some years back a prominent senator was fond of saying with regard to the relatively modest lobbying influence of the day: "If I can't take their money and drink their whiskey, and then vote against them, I shouldn't be here." That was then. And then campaigns cost much less than they do today. Few if any can now claim to take their money and drink their whiskey and vote against them. Anyone who does will soon find closed wallets and fleeing contributors.

Campaign funds now go to feed an army of consultants (or "strategists" in the coinage of the day), media advisors, media producers, television-time buyers, speechwriters, schedulers, advance specialists, crowd raisers, and more specialized campaign bells and whistles than everyday citizens can imagine. Campaigning is a major industry now that consumes hundreds of millions of dollars and, in national campaigns, billions of dollars. Almost all of it goes to the media, the same media whose commentators regularly deplore the costs of campaigns.

The headquarters of the permanent campaign industry in Washington are but a stone's throw, if that, from the offices of the lobbying firms. The treasurers of most campaigns have only to funnel the checks from lobbyist-bundlers (those who collect bundles of checks) into the accounts of the campaign-management companies. It is a great hydra-headed monster, one that is rapidly devouring American democracy.

The significant issue is the effect of this relatively recent conversion of a democratic process to a major industry that devours money. That industry and all it represents is a departure from the American ideal that is different not only in scale but also in kind.

We are not the same country we started out to be. We cannot conduct our political process the way we are doing in the twenty-first century and claim to adhere to our earliest principles. We must decide who we are. And if that decision is to restore our highest ideals, then major changes must be made in the way we elect our presidents and our members of Congress.

THE REPUBLIC
OF CONSCIENCE:
A MANIFESTO

Reconciliation of our current political structures and policies with our original founding beliefs requires some form of manifesto—a statement of fundamental principles relevant to the current age. According to the thesis presented here, it is possible to remain true to the principles of our founders and their founding documents, both in the way we govern ourselves at home and in the way we conduct our relations with other nations, even in a new age characterized by dramatic new realities. What follows is an attempt to outline what those principles are, both domestic and foreign, and how our conduct based upon them might be structured.

The pragmatic fallacy occurs when expediency, the need to solve an immediate or current problem, causes us and our policy makers to adopt the most convenient approach, one that may or may not be consistent with our basic principles.

Pragmatism, practicality in problem solving, is required as circumstances and realities change, and they constantly do. Problems arise, however, when nations or individuals lose their compass and their bearings, when they too easily and too willingly abandon principle just to get by and move on.

Let's consider some examples. A needed energy supply is discovered on public land, a wilderness area, for example, and the immediate demand for that energy would require violation of our responsibility to future generations—"our posterity"—for whom that area was preserved. The pragmatic solution is to develop the energy supply. The principled position is to look elsewhere for alternative energy supplies or adopt conservation measures.

Another example might occur if a friendly foreign nation, an ally, is faced with a threat on its borders, a threat not shared by the United States, and our ally requests U.S. military intervention to help eliminate the threat. The pragmatic approach would be to send an expeditionary force to help the ally and, at the same time, demonstrate what some call "strength." The principled approach is to urge caution against unnecessary foreign adventures and seek to support the ally without the commitment of U.S. troops.

A further example occurs almost daily in today's globalized world. We are buying products from a foreign country that is investing in government bonds that finance our national debt, but it has a miserable record on human rights. The pragmatic approach says that debt financing and consumer satisfaction are paramount. The principled position points out that we cannot preach human rights as central to our foreign policy while turning a blind eye when immediate gratification requires.

These and hundreds of other real-world instances present themselves routinely and constantly to the policy makers who are responsible to the American electorate. Clearly, we weave in and around these dilemmas, and as often as not, we do what is expedient and pragmatic.

But when we do so, we sacrifice principle and moral authority. Older nations less under the world's scrutiny have long since done what is required to get by. The European foreign policy phrase for this pragmatic expediency is "realpolitik," realistic politics. In post–World War II America that approach took root in our politics and foreign policy: Do what is necessary to protect our national security, promote our leadership position, and demonstrate our superior strength. It is not meant to be pejorative to call this the Europeanization of American foreign policy.

In some cases, realism served us well when one form or another of absolutism arose in U.S. political circles. Some wanted the U.S. to intervene routinely and unilaterally when human rights were being violated. Others, in Iraq, for example, urged military invasion to overthrow a "cruel dictator" and establish a U.S. military and political base of considerable size in the troubled regions of the Middle East. Realists, on the other hand, essentially accept the world as it is and seek to establish workable relations, most significantly in the former Soviet Union, that protect and promote American interests.

The dark side of "realpolitik," however, began to surface in the 1970s with the disclosures of clandestine operations to overthrow troublesome governments, to suborn foreign journalists, to penetrate trade organizations, and generally to conduct the Cold War, including the assassination of foreign leaders, in the back alleys of the world. With long-overdue congressional inquiries, triggered in part by Watergate, Americans began to discover that the nation they believed to be principled, the one taught in high school civics classes as better than older nations, had become like all the rest and had adopted policies and practices that clashed with who we believe ourselves to be.

The Cold War offers an example of where our proclaimed principles required us to live up to them at home. The world had divided itself between the democratic West, led by the United States, and the Communist Bloc, led by the Soviet Union. These two sides confronted each other on a daily basis, especially in Europe, but found their ideological competition in the so-called Third World: Latin America, Africa, and Asia. It goes without saying that two superpower coalitions composed primarily of white-skinned people were competing in the two-thirds of the world where skins were darker.

The Soviet Union made sure that these three vast areas of the world were made familiar with racial discrimination in the United States in the 1940s, '50s, and '60s. Foreign policy, at least as far as the civil rights movement was concerned, required us to practice our Constitutional principles in terms of racial equality if we were to win the hearts and minds of Latin Americans, Africans, and Asians. Pragmatism and principle coincided and we had no choice but to do the right thing and try to become who we claimed to be.

From this historical example we can begin to see the path toward reconciliation of practice and belief, between pragmatism in problem solving on a daily basis and principle in our conduct at home and abroad. The challenge is to formulate a manifesto that represents a framework for that reconciliation. Separate sets of principles are required for our domestic and foreign conduct.

AMERICA AT HOME

For almost three centuries Americans have struggled to accommodate the interests of a commonwealth with a capitalist economic system. There has never been a serious effort to convert the United States to socialism or widespread state ownership. There have been continuing efforts, even today, to convert much of our publicly owned resources to private ownership and development.

The resources of the commonwealth include public transportation systems, interstate highways, canal systems, and seaports; public land and resource holdings largely in the West, forests, mineral deposits, parks, monuments, and wilderness areas; mints and coinage; a judicial system and court structures; public education systems; and security agencies at home and abroad. These and many more represent the resources and interests of the commonwealth, all those things that belong to our citizens in common.

There has been a perpetual effort to privatize natural resources, especially those found in Western states where the national government is a consequential landlord. In recent years this has been paralleled by efforts to privatize transportation systems with corporate contractors collecting tolls in exchange for ownership and maintenance of the systems. What should and should not be administered by public agencies on behalf of all citizens and without a profit motive will remain contested in the political competition between the private interests of corporations and shareholders and nonprofit public institutions.

However this struggle is resolved on a case-by-case basis, it is imperative that the public interest be protected. Once again, the interests of our posterity, specifically included in our Constitution's preamble, must be factored into all decisions. Sufficient unto the day are the profits thereof. The charters of few if any private corporations include concern for the well-being of future generations. The principle involved is generational accountability. We are morally obligated and Constitutionally mandated to consider the impact of our current decisions on our progeny. What might represent the possibility of financial profit today might not also protect the future interests of those to whom we are accountable.

Two principles are involved: the proper protection and preservation of the institutions and resources of the commonwealth, and the incorporation of the interests of future generations in our administration of the public good.

Citizens must perform their duties to protect their rights.

Given their extensive education in the history and theory of the republic, our founders placed at the top of the requirements for the perpetuation of the new American Republic the quality of civic virtue, the obligation of citizen involvement in the public life of the nation.

It is significant that this ancient concept has fallen into disrepair and disuse. We Americans have always vacillated between a sense of laissez-faire—leave me alone—and patriotism. These cycles are usually marked by crises: Let me know if the country needs me, otherwise leave me alone. In modern times we reached a zenith of patriotism during World War II when eleven million members of the Greatest Generation donned military uniforms, rationing was instituted for civilians (albeit with a considerable black market), flags were flown, liberty bonds were sold, patriotic music permeated the airwaves, schoolchildren participated in scrap drives, and John Philip Sousa marches were heard across the land.

Clearly, this level of national cohesion is impossible to sustain absent a threat to national survival. So, in more or less normal times, everyday Americans want their government to leave them alone. Despite our espousing a foreign policy of democratic values, voter levels, especially in off-year or nonnational elections, are remarkably low. The other principal duty of male citizens, a military draft, was abandoned after Vietnam. And there is sustained resistance to payment of national taxes even to support a social safety net that large majorities of working- and middle-class Americans expect.

But our founders were deeply concerned that without widespread civic virtue and citizen engagement, an uncorrupted republic could not be sustained. And there is plenty of evidence in history for this conviction. Disregard, now bordering with some justification on contempt, of government is rampant. Men and women of talent and quality reject the ideal of public service. Consequently, the national government in Washington is now captive to a permanent professional class that moves in and out of the corridors of power depending on the outcome of national elections, and when out of power, it stays in Washington awaiting a restoration of a particular political party while earning large sums lobbying a Rolodex network of political acquaintances. This may be a new system of governance, but it is by no means a republic—and it's certainly not the republic created by our founders.

Populist protestors of the right (Tea Party) or left (Occupiers) in the tradition of the late nineteenth-century populists may be a form of civic virtue, but this is far from the ideal our founders and ancient republicans had in mind. Indeed, properly exercised, civic virtue by everyday citizens would preclude the necessity of such marginal populism.

The rise of today's permanent political class is a phenomenon of the past three decades. It is characterized by the professionalization of elective politics, with candidates for national or statewide office finding it necessary to hire professional fund-raisers, campaign managers, media consultants who rotate between selling consumer products and selling candidates, time buyers experienced in placing television advertising, schedulers and organizers, and even opposition research specialists to ferret out an opponent's missteps.

Most of all, it is the nexus of fund-raisers and lobbyists that is destroying American democracy and the original ideal of our Republic. Unlike even thirty short years ago, senators (and, of course, representatives) today allocate a certain number of hours a day to the demeaning exercise of telephone appeals for contributions. This occurs not just in election years but *throughout a six-year term*. Needless to say, the hours given to fund-raising at this level are hours not spent conducting the public's business for which they are elected.

It is too much to say that we now find ourselves in this massively destructive political cul-de-sac simply because the vast majority of citizens lack civic virtue and don't pay attention. It is not too much to say that there is some connection between the two. This is why our founders paid so much attention to the republican quality of resisting corruption. A republic given over to narrow, special, and personal interests, as ours now is, soon becomes something other than a republic. Inattention to civic virtue—participation, involvement, and concern—creates a vacuum inevitably filled by corruption and corrupters.

Likewise, a corrupt system such as ours has become soon makes itself inaccessible to citizens concerned with the common good. This cycle must be broken sooner rather than later if our Republic is to be renewed and we are to keep faith both with our founders and future generations.

If asked their opinion on this matter, members of the permanent professional political class would say that our country and its government is a conglomeration of group interests, that balancing these often competing interests is the day-to-day job of legislators and executives. Give a little here; give a little there.

This is a fundamentally flawed understanding of our nation and its creation. It flies in the face of virtually all the writings and speeches of those who created the United States and who took part in the Constitutional debates, wrote *The Federalist Papers*, and corresponded between themselves as our Constitution was taking shape. The principles of the republic were crucial to them. They did not use language lightly. They knew exactly what they were doing. They had a range of options, often heatedly debated, about institutions, structures, and methods, and they purposely and carefully laid out a system for creating and balancing national political power along the lines first established in ancient Athens and Rome. And they repeatedly warned against tampering with those institutions and structures and the principles upon which they were based so as not to risk losing their unique creation.

We are perilously close to doing exactly that.

Contrary to prevailing opinion in Washington's permanent professional political class, there is something called "the national interest." This is not a phrase from a political-science textbook. The national interest is tangible and it is real. It is separate from and superior to the conglomeration of special group interests that dominates our politics today.

The national interest requires that primary priority be given to the institutions and resources of the commonwealth, all those things we own together and preserve for our posterity, our generational accountability and moral responsibility to Americans who will follow, and the well-being of the nation. These are not abstractions. These concerns are as real as, and more important than, the concerns of individual industries, business groups, cause-specific organizations, particular interest groups of one kind or another, and all the lists of organizations that take up many pages in the Washington, D.C., telephone directory.

The permanent professional political class has lost sight of the national interest. Many of its members could not articulate a definition of the national interest if compelled to do so. That is not their concern. Their concern is first and foremost for power—who has it, how it may be captured, and how it can be monetized. They are consumed by money, money for campaigns and the mountains of money produced by the lobbying for the very narrow interests our founders warned would destroy our republic. The lobby for the national interest should be the people we elect.

The national interest can only survive in the individual minds and hearts of Americans who care for their country today, who care even more for the nation they will leave their children, and who are willing to take the time and trouble to protect both.

For the restoration of civic virtue—citizen participation in government—the citizen must first believe her government to be honest. Honesty here is meant to include not simply its public statements but also the basic integrity of its processes and the individuals who legislate and administer.

Arguably, nothing in recent times has undermined citizen confidence in governmental integrity more than revelations of the wholesale collection of private communications among citizens by the National Security Agency and other intelligence organizations. But this follows a dismal pattern in the second half of the twentieth century.

Many were encouraged to believe that the assassinations of President John F. Kennedy, Senator Robert Kennedy, and Reverend Martin Luther King, Jr., could not have been carried out without some involvement of individuals or organizations of the United States government. Soon thereafter came the release of secret documents from the Vietnam War that confirmed doubts about the war's outcome by those conducting the war even while they were repeatedly convincing the American people that we were winning. Then, on top of that, came Watergate, the systematic manipulation of the American political system by a president and the top levels of his administration.

Thereafter, journalistic rewards were offered for disclosure, by any means devised, of the private lives of presidents and political figures, with varying degrees of accuracy and verifiability. The duty of selecting leaders shifted from the people to the press. It is one thing for the people to know the emperor has no clothes. It is another for the media to peek in the windows of his private home to prove it.

Beginning in the twenty-first century, this pattern of false and misleading statements on matters of life and death resumed with the invasion of Iraq and an expanded war in Afghanistan that were based on a "war on terrorism." That Iraq had nothing to do with terrorism was proved only after the fact—that is, after our invasion.

None of this contributed to citizen confidence in government. Indeed, it had just the opposite effect. There have been a number of periods of traditional money-under-the-table, quid-pro-quo kinds of corruption in the past. But from the 1960s onward there is little parallel in American history for this repeated assault on citizen confidence.

One further factor contributes to widespread public skepticism. That is the rise of the partisan media and especially its public cynicism. The most egregious example, of course, is Fox News, which cynically hides behind a grossly inaccurate promise of being "fair and balanced" while it systematically encourages the notion that our own government by its very nature is evil—with the possible exception of when it is occupied by the network's political partisans.

Citizen confidence in government also requires that the government be just. Being just, fair, and equitable requires more than the maintenance of a judicial system, even one that is beyond reproach. A just government administers a just society. A just society possesses a conscience, a sense of decency and humanity for all its citizens. This sense is often called social justice.

Corrupted governments, those pursuing narrow interests rather than the common good, do not take kindly to those who point out injustice. We often call those prophetic voices reformers and they are honored more in their deaths than in their lives. The history of American social reform traces from the colonies up through Martin Luther King, Jr., and Robert Kennedy and usually focuses reluctant attention on unfairness, inequality, poverty, and all those social ills we call injustice.

Those who seek justice, especially in societies distracted by materialism and wealth accumulation, are often lonely voices, marginalized for focusing reluctant attention on the gap between what is and what ought to be and for prodding the sense of injustice dormant in us all. André Schwarz-Bart wrote a brilliant novel about such voices called *The Last of the Just*. He recalls an ancient Jewish legend that at all times and in all societies there are a very small number of people called the Just. They bear a heavy burden, one they do not particularly welcome, to remind us all that injustice is all around us. Those whose focus is on power and wealth in government and business would rather rely on some vague slogan like "A thousand points of light" than deal with injustices that permeate most societies. An unjust government will not maintain the confidence of its people.

A former Senate colleague, Gaylord Nelson of Wisconsin, was fond of saying that our national security was dependent on a sound dollar, secure borders, and the confidence of the people in their government. All three, but especially the third, are now in question, and none can be restored by nuclear weapons or the attraction of foreign capital.

Our political leaders of all ideologies and both parties have a duty to restore confidence and they cannot do so by mounting election campaigns that focus exclusively on how dreadful circumstances are in Washington. The burden of restoring confidence rests also on parents, teachers, business leaders, religious figures, and many others to promote civic virtue, citizen duty, and the values of public service. The failure is not just in the political arena; it is throughout our society.

"Ask what you can do for your country" was the iconic phrase that awakened a sense of participation in public life among my generation. In my small law school class alone were future governors, senators, federal judges, treasury secretaries and other cabinet officers. That challenge has not been heard since. Indeed, twenty years after that inaugural address, a new president said, "The government is the problem," hardly a clarion call to public service. And today we reap the result of that appeal to cynicism.

Elected and appointed officials seem smaller in stature and vision now. Those citizens with the most to contribute refuse to accept routine media hazing and contentious partisan appointment delays. The shrinking of political leaders, men and women, is as much cultural as it is political. Television anchors, movie stars, and business leaders have all shrunk. Where have you gone Walter Cronkite, or Lee Iacocca, or Gary Cooper, or Walter Lippmann? A recent article in the *New York Times* on the triumph of the adolescent culture observed: "It seems that, in doing away with patriarchal authority, we have also, perhaps unwittingly, killed off all the grown-ups . . . nobody knows how to be a grown-up anymore. Adulthood . . . has become conceptually untenable."

The manifesto for America at home, one that places our pragmatic policy making to address the realities of the day in the context of our nation's abiding principles, may thus be summarized as follows:

We are a commonwealth with public institutions and resources, in which citizens have duties to preserve their rights and promote civic virtue; since we are a commonwealth characterized by civic virtue, our national interest and common good supersede all the narrow interests; and citizen confidence in government must be restored through public integrity in order to recapture civic virtue and sustain the commonwealth.

AMERICA IN THE WORLD

Despite their concern for the contentious history of Europe and the dangers involvement in European turmoil represented for the new nation, our founders were not only nation builders, they were also diplomats. John Adams, Benjamin Franklin, Thomas Jefferson, James Monroe, and many others occupied American embassies in London, Paris, Madrid, and elsewhere during the period of the Confederation, the Revolutionary War, and beyond our Constitutional federation. They understood that amicable relations, even with nations that did not necessarily wish us well, were vital to our survival.

Disengagement from European power politics and endless conflict by no means represented isolationism. From the colonial era onward, early Americans were engaged in trade. Wealth in natural resources could not replace the need for finished products unobtainable in the early colonies and states. Jefferson brought back fine French wine with him on his return from Paris and sought thereafter, with limited success, to replicate them at Monticello. The otherwise prudent Franklin reveled in European society and was lionized for it.

The founders were by and large sophisticated men of the world but were cautious about political entanglements that could impede the crucial need for the new Republic to get its roots firmly down. It would take the age of Theodore

Roosevelt and his world-touring "great white fleet" to signal the United States' intentions to be considered a consequential world power, but even then Woodrow Wilson and Franklin Roosevelt faced considerable conservative opposition to military engagement in both world wars. Full Europeanization of American foreign policy would await the arrival of Henry Kissinger as national security advisor in the age of Nixon.

A manifesto for America in the world, however, will feature our continued commitment to membership in the global community of nations, perhaps best symbolized by the presence of the United Nations headquarters on our shores, but will focus attention on more careful deployment of America's military forces. Indeed, if America's role in the world has exceeded the founders' intent, it is in the militarization of our foreign policy and the tendency of successive administrations to adopt an expeditionary approach to the world's problems.

A significant factor in this trend has been the willingness of the Western democratic world to let the American soldier, financed by the American taxpayer, provide security for it and as much of the rest of the world as we care to police while at the same time reserving the hypocritical right to denounce our aggressive behavior. Likewise, United States policy makers have been consistently willing to accept the costs of this burden rather than rely on allies that may, or may not, show up when threats arise.

Now in the age of globalization there is little if any risk of

American isolationism. In light of the indecisive outcomes in Afghanistan and Iraq, and the real chance both nations will revert to ancient sectarian and tribal conflict, there is understandable citizen resistance to significant deployment of U.S. military forces absent a direct attack from foreign sources. But even as neoconservatives sought to demonize the People's Republic of China to fill the vacuum created by the collapse of Soviet Communism and thus justify continued Cold War–style vigilance and huge defense budgets, trade relations with China skyrocketed and dependence on Chinese debt financing became crucial to our fiscal health.

Given the increasingly intricate trade relations of the U.S. worldwide, the wholesale transfer of U.S. manufacturing to Asia and elsewhere, the globalization of our professional (legal, accounting, and so forth) services and financial sectors, and the creation of instant communication networks, there is little if any chance of American retrenchment. Globalization, indeed, has led to the commercialization of the U.S. diplomatic system. Since the Clinton administration, large segments of our diplomatic networks are now devoted to providing assistance to U.S. companies seeking entrée to foreign markets.

Aside from a lingering security role in the age of terrorism and large-scale economic involvement abroad, the post–Cold War era has yet to yield a clearly defined U.S. role in the world. The period between 1991 when the Soviet Union collapsed and 2001 with the 9/11 attacks did not produce that new definition. The subsequent George W. Bush years featured a "war on terrorism" that no longer seems sufficient to describe our purpose. And the most recent Obama years have been guided by a risk-avoidance effort not to do "stupid stuff."

In part, this reflects the absence of a definable enemy. It is much easier to unite our nation against an enemy than to unite us behind a common good. Thus, the foreign policy establishment produces reams of theories about how to define our foreign policy and our role in the world. Amid this confusion and lack of direction, reversion to the basic principle of our founders offers a starting point.

We seek to be left alone and will not trouble others. Do not tread on us and we will not tread on you. No entangling alliances. Though it may seem simplistic, there is guidance for America's role in the world in the analogy to the relationship of neighbors. The best neighbors are friendly, helpful, and cooperative on matters of common interest but reticent about meddling in each other's family affairs. Though infinitely more complicated, the relations of nations need not be much more different in principle.

This approach based on our founders' principles is a clear departure from U.S. foreign policy of the past sixty-five years. Power operates in several traditional categories: economic, political, and military. To a degree unprecedented in U.S. history, our foreign policy during the Cold War and terrorist years has been heavily military, and even today when political figures demand that we demonstrate "strength," this is known to mean the use of force. Military power has become the instinctive default category for dealing with international problems.

Circumstances, primarily fiscal limits, are requiring us to question this instinct and search for alternative approaches to international relations and frictions. Western democracies can and should assume a much greater role in collective security, even at the expense of U.S. command. Our security problems are increasingly collective—terrorism especially—and solutions must be multinational. Our special forces are the best in the world, but others can augment and supplement them.

Likewise, intelligence relating to collective threats must be more readily shared. We do not have to spend $40 billion annually collecting and analyzing intelligence on common dangers when others can assume some of this burden. Of course, such cooperation might require us not to spy on our allies.

This suggests our post–World War II security alliances, especially the North Atlantic Treaty Organization (NATO), will not be abandoned. But it makes imminent sense to reorganize and reform those alliances twenty-five years after the end of the Cold War, to take into account new twenty-first-century realities. Times change. Circumstances change. New purposes and structures for old organizations are required to maintain relevance. Who are we defending ourselves against? What role does each partner-country play? How will security burdens be fairly shared?

It is nothing short of astounding how many traditionally local and national concerns have become international in scope in the twenty-first century. Climate change, pandemics, and ocean pollution all threaten the global commons. The critical global infrastructure now includes financial, communications, energy distribution, and transportation systems on which all nations depend. Isolation is not an option for anyone any longer.

Because the collapse of the Soviet Union left us without an enemy or even a peer competitor, many U.S. defense and foreign policy experts feared U.S. retreat from the world. As with China, efforts were made to construct a new enemy, even if one was not apparent. This pattern of thinking is contrary to our history and the place in the world our founders saw for their new nation. Throughout its history, the United States has not required an enemy to be engaged, but not entangled, with the world. We would be very mistaken to continue, contrary to John Quincy Adams's warning, to go abroad seeking monsters to destroy.

Most nations of the world do not wish us ill and many wish us well, including the Chinese who believe enough in the strength of our currency to invest hundreds of billions of dollars in our bonds. Ill-wishers now are composed of radical religious fundamentalists, ethnic nationalists, and murderous tribes and gangs. We have dealt with them before, most notably at our beginning when President Jefferson sent warships to quell the Barbary pirates during his first term. In 1832, President James Monroe issued a doctrine that put the entire Western Hemisphere off-limits to European colonial powers. We would not meddle in their affairs and they were not to meddle in the affairs of our southern neighbors that were beginning to throw off the colonial yoke.

It is now timely to question the entire structure of United States foreign policy since World War II, the purpose not being to retreat or isolate ourselves. That would be impossible in the world of the twenty-first century. The purpose would be to look on this century's new realities with a cold eye and redefine where we can and cannot be helpful to ourselves and our allies. So-called pivots to Asia and so forth assume a role grander than is required of us. A nation in the business of pivoting is a nation in need of an enduring strategy and new bearings. Ballerinas pivot and the United States does not resemble a ballerina.

Since the end of the Cold War, we have engaged in so-called nation-building exercises in various venues with only limited results. We supply large amounts of money, only meager amounts of which escape the clutches of the powerful and produce tangible results for everyday people. Meanwhile, efforts to rebuild America languish. Transportation, education, and communication dollars cannot be found. It is a curiosity of the age why conservative politicians like to build other nations but not their own.

America's founders, schooled in the discipline of the classic republic, feared a large standing army and navy. Throughout history, those became havens for mercenaries and the instruments of dictators. Our Constitution clearly authorizes Congress to provide for an army and a navy, and made the civilian president their commander in chief. Military officers would take their orders from civilian leadership and their forces would be financed by the representatives of the people.

The principal defense of our shores rested in the hands of the citizen militia that was mentioned three times in the Constitution and armed for this purpose according to the Second Amendment. In direct opposition to our defenses since World War II, the standing army was to defend our shores until the minutemen could organize and arrive. Now roles are reversed. We send expeditionary forces of professional soldiers to Afghanistan and Iraq, and support them with state national guards composed of citizen soldiers who are the descendants of the original militia.

The front line of our homeland defense should be the National Guard, men and women trained and equipped and locally based who are more readily available, and Constitutionally authorized, to repel and respond to domestic attacks. In military terms, they are "forward deployed" at home.

Were we to go abroad seeking monsters to destroy, our founders knew we would need a much larger standing army to do so—and what is that army to do in peacetime between expeditions? The cul-de-sac into which we have entered is best summarized by the question of then Secretary of State Madeleine Albright to then General Colin Powell: "Why do we have this big army if we're not going to use it?"

Three successive administrations since the end of the Cold War have neglected to use this period for the serious restructuring of our military forces for defensive missions and occasional small-scale special forces operations planned on a carefully defined basis. Our policy makers and strategists, including presidents, would do well to spend more time studying military history.

Creative thinking might produce a new approach to security. Throughout most of the second half of the twentieth century, the U.S. national security strategy was to contain Communism. In the first decade of the twenty-first century, the national security strategy became a war on terrorism. Neither is relevant now as a central organizing principle for dealing with this century's new realities. Instead, our new strategy should be the reduction of threats.

Slowing the projected growth of military spending, at the

very least, will be included in future deficit reductions. But applying arbitrary across-the-board cuts in defense absent a clearer picture of the central purpose of our security strategy would be foolish at best and destructive at worst. Big budgets produce bad defense policies. Arbitrary budget cuts will produce even worse ones.

Principal among threat-reduction measures is controlling weapons of mass destruction and the prevention of any such weapons from proliferating or falling into the hands of terrorist organizations. There are other threats, however, that require sustained attention as well. These include failed and failing states, cyber attacks, pandemics, climate destabilization, religious fundamentalism, tribalism, ethnic nationalism, and a variety of other realities that characterize this new century.

Throughout the second half of the twentieth and the early part of the twenty-first centuries, the United States relied on military superiority to respond to national and international threats. The nature of warfare and the character of conflict are changing, however, and, as we are learning from our current long wars, military superiority as defined in the Westphalian era of the nation-state is proving less effective. Vastly shortened warning and response time, the emergence of non-state actors, and the spread of unconventional conflict now mean that traditional large-scale military power is much less effective both as a deterrent and as a response. Much more effective will be the reduction of threats *before* they become immediate and difficult, if not impossible, to manage.

Rather than seeking to control international upheavals and chaos through traditional diplomatic and political means and, should those fail, resorting to overwhelming military power, we will now find it necessary to identify evildoers before they act, break up threatening networks, anticipate disruption, isolate violence, deny targets of opportunity, and be smarter than the new agents of destruction.

In a word, our central strategy must be to drastically limit opportunities for violence *before* it occurs. This strategy requires undercutting the motivation of disruptive actors, restricting their opportunity to act, and shrinking the resources and capabilities of those inclined to disruption. It also means applying more sophisticated anticipatory response planning to nonmilitary threats such as Hurricane Katrina and the Gulf of Mexico oil spill.

Since the strategy of anticipation and threat reduction will never be absolutely perfect, military forces, especially special forces and targeted capabilities, must be shaped to deal with those threats that avoid or escape total confinement. But, by virtue of threat-reduction efforts, these will be smaller threats that can be dealt with by smaller combat units and more targeted firepower.

This new strategy turns traditional military thinking on its head. Rather than wait until threats become massive and are exercised, all resources should go into preventing these threats from reaching large-scale proportions and into keeping them within more manageable parameters, especially in a century already marked by fast-moving events.

Thus, a project begun toward the close of the Cold War to reduce nuclear and other arsenals as a means of reducing the threats they had previously represented should now become the centerpiece of a new national strategy. The Defense Threat Reduction Agency at the Department of Defense was created as a consolidation of Cold War arms-control and disarmament-monitoring agencies. It is increasingly tasked with coordinating the control of weapons of mass destruction. But it also supports response efforts involving Japan's Fukushima nuclear reactor and other nonmilitary threats.

Much of the confusion over the nature of security in the twenty-first century emerges from the absence of a peer competitor, such as the former Soviet Union, which offered a focus for our security preparations. But the idea of threat reduction, provided by an era of arms control, can and should take on new meaning in an era of more dispersed and amorphous military and nonmilitary threats.

Lacking a central organizing principle for our security, we should take the core idea from an agency created to wind down the Cold War and broaden the principle of threat reduction into the centerpiece of a new anticipatory, proactive national security strategy.

||||||||||||||||||

I f the founders made one thing clear throughout their discourses, it was that the United States did not seek to create an empire except for, as the noted historian Gordon Wood writes, "an empire of liberty" that would stretch across the continent of North America. This continental power was built by expedition, exploration, military confrontation (with Mexico), negotiated purchase (with France), and occupation. The founders saw no contradiction between their desire to occupy a continent they came to believe belonged to them and their resistance to foreign entanglements that conquest of "foreign" territory might require.

Since the end of World War II, the United States has found itself walking a fine line that separates resistance to domination on the part of others from the use of political and military power by the United States itself. At its best, this duality can be expressed as follows: We will resist hegemony without seeking hegemony.

At its worst, particularly during the darkest days of the Cold War, we supported or imposed dictators who were friendly to us and the West (as we did in Iran). This form of control by puppets was seen by others as just another form of imperialism led in the shadows by the CIA. Most Americans, especially those steeped in early American history, turned a blind eye. The ideological struggle of the Cold War justified expediency over principle at every turn.

A nation founded on a principle of no foreign entanglements found itself in the second half of the twentieth century entangled virtually everywhere, from tiny islands in the Caribbean to the jungles of Vietnam. The key foreign policy phrase and guiding organizing principle was protecting our "national security interests." This phrase was considered by foreign policy elites to be self-explanatory and self-justifying, and it was a code phrase that encompassed a multitude of sins. It did not require explanation. A president, secretary of state, or national security advisor had merely to utter the phrase "national security interest" and what followed was justified. It was left purposely vague and undefined, especially when it came to protecting foreign oil supplies upon which we were then critically dependent.

Toward the end of his life when he was seeking support for his new internationalism, President Franklin Roosevelt said that the well-being of the United States "is dependent on the well-being of other nations." As this country was the sole remaining economic and military power in the world at midcentury, this was surely true, and the early guiding directive against foreign entanglements was replaced by the Marshall Plan, a Douglas MacArthur regency in Japan, the United Nations, NATO, a large and growing panoply of U.S. foreign military bases and a dozen or more large-scale naval task forces, and ever-expanding embassies. Virtually overnight there were very few foreign venues in which we were not entangled.

Despite our far-flung military installations, many of which, it must be said, were welcomed by local authorities as crucial to their own security, and despite Cold War espionage wars with the Soviets, now largely replaced by electronic surveillance (including of our allies), the United States has largely avoided the imperial role. A fair assessment of America's role in the world would conclude that we have made our fair share of political and diplomatic mistakes but have refused to seek regional hegemony.

In too many instances, however, pragmatism has trumped principle, and successive American administrations have made up our actions on a case-by-case basis as we went along. Over the decades, various slogans—such as "We are the indispensable nation"—have operated as a substitute for genuine policy and consistent strategy, all while we sought to justify America's overwhelming global presence while assuring the world we were not the new imperialists. And, despite the expedient use of proxies and puppets during the Cold War, we have been remarkably free of the historic tendency of dominant nations to colonize foreign countries, that is, so long as they remained compliant.

In recent years foreign policy experts have predicted the

rise of counterbalancing powers—first Japan, now China, and some say regional powers such as Brazil, Russia, and India—to offset the U.S. presence around the world. This may or may not prove true, but decades will have to pass before we will know. Many Americans, tired of wars in Iraq and Afghanistan, would welcome such a development. The American character seems not to welcome endless international engagements, certainly not those that lead to military conflict and occur during periods of economic instability at home.

But huge changes in the international landscape since the end of the Cold War will require a new approach, one not clearly developed at this stage, to rationalize U.S. presence in the world. Globalization and the information revolution are the most dominant new economic and political realities. In the security realm, the fragmentation of fragile nation-states, the former Yugoslavia, for example, and the outbreak of ancient sectarian rivalries and hatreds across the Middle East have introduced the rise of ethnic nationalism, religious fundamentalism, tribalism, and the rise of criminal states, as in Mexico and Central America.

Religious fundamentalism in the Middle East and elsewhere has resorted to eleventh-century terrorism as its particular tactic, a tactic not aimed at the United States exclusively. Destruction of the decadent and imperialistic West is its aim, with the late Osama bin Laden preaching the importance of destroying the U.S. economy, not merely its tall buildings.

The more cancerous of the fundamentalists morph into ever-changing shapes and forms. Virtually overnight the previously unheard-of army of the Islamic State arose in and around the Syrian civil war in the summer of 2014 and migrated into a fragmenting Iraq almost unchecked. Experts warned that it has recruited fundamentalists with Western passports who are capable, therefore, of entering the U.S. and elsewhere through routine customs and passport controls, not by means of hijacked airplanes.

Even the mighty United States cannot address this threat alone. The networks of intelligence collection and analysis and multinational special forces will have to be expanded substantially. They will have to be versed in the warfare of the future (and the ancient past), hand-to-hand combat; surprise high-risk penetration of hostile territories; assassinations; and agent recruitment. This unconventional, irregular combat will have to have the support of new technologies such as the drones that are presently carrying out some assassinations.

What Washington, Madison, Adams, Jefferson, and others would make of all this might prove an interesting parlor game. Those clinging to the policy of no foreign entanglements would advocate the most strenuous kind of border control. Withdraw to the homeland and hunker down. Those more internationally minded would support the continued effort to consolidate like-minded peoples in an effort to isolate and then decimate treacherous fundamentalist organizations. Whatever the outcome of that debate, it is safe to conclude that the threat of religious fundamentalism to the American home-land will continue for the foreseeable future and, as the U.S. Commission on National Security for the Twenty-First Century concluded as early as 1999, "Americans will die on American soil, possibly in large numbers."

The dawn of globalization as we know it today came some-time in the 1970s. We awoke one morning around then to find that the cars in our driveways were manufactured in Germany or Japan, countries that only three short decades before were our destitute enemies. The labels on our clothing bore Asian brands. Our watches, television sets, shoes, appliances, and almost everything else needed on a daily basis began to arrive on our shores in containers from somewhere else carried on cargo ships that seemed to increase in size almost weekly.

The political response to this was substantial pressure to adopt protectionist legislation for our auto, steel, textile, and other manufacturing industries. But by then or shortly there-after, the increasing middle classes in developed and develop-ing nations, fueled by the windfall from American purchases of their products, desired Boeing jets, telecommunication sys-tems, and Microsoft software. America's traditional manu-facturing sector in the East was under competitive assault and in decline, with consequent job losses and urban decay, while the new information, communications, and air-transportation sectors in the West were flourishing.

Thus, America's foreign policy is now driven to a large degree by the new realities of globalization. Enormous political energy goes into the negotiation of fair-trade rules to prevent other nations, especially China, from currency manipulation and mercantilism that puts a thumb on the scales of trade. The difficult news is that international competition characterized by goods produced under low-wage conditions, and therefore less expensive than U.S. manufactured products, causes large-scale unemployment and the economic devastation of whole communities. The better news is that the intricate networks of international commerce substantially decrease the likelihood of a conflict that escalates into nation-state warfare. A sufficient number of U.S. policy makers remember the history of a century ago when rampant protectionism led to confrontation and then warfare.

Not only has consumer trade dramatically expanded, trade in services, insurance, health care, communications, information, and many other sectors has substantially also benefited the United States. Likewise, the professions of law and accounting are now internationalized. American lawyers now find more in common with their Indian, British, and Italian counterparts, and now partners, than they do with their fellow citizens outside their profession. And, of course, all are familiar with the migration of "back offices" to Asia, where skilled guidance is provided by young Indians and Bangladeshis to correct television or telephone malfunctions or sort out unpaid bills.

All of this must naturally have political consequences. Intricate international networks for products, services, and support have been created, facilitated by greatly expanded air travel and instant communications. Politicians and policy makers on all continents must respond to and more often than not support these networks. Thus, politics is increasingly internationalized. The United States usually finds itself leading the way, with the exception for attempts to protect special interests.

Divisions now are less between nation-states and more between haves and have-nots. Poor people have more in common with poor people everywhere than prosperous people have in common with poor people anywhere. Relative wealth and abject poverty often live almost side by side in many countries, the difference being that those with wealth now form their own republics of wealth in privately protected and gated enclaves located on hilltops in or near almost every major urban area worldwide.

The growth in the private security industry has been astronomical in recent decades. Even ethnic communities in the United States, such as the Korean business community in Los Angeles, have private police forces to protect their businesses. Wealthy individuals routinely hire bodyguards for themselves, their families, and their homes. Major businesses hire security contractors to protect their facilities and key employees throughout international networks. Former CIA and FBI agents systematically join private security firms upon retirement—if they are not already commentators on television networks.

Wealthy individuals and major business are thus protecting themselves from major and minor crimes committed by the poor but also from fundamentalist threats directed by those using terrorism as a tactic. They are visualizing threats from below and from the side. Even as globalization was opening markets; internationalizing finance, commerce, and markets; and integrating trading networks, its encroachment on traditional fundamentalist cultures fed resentments and anger at liberal values and practices (especially in the movie, television, and music industries) and encouraged violent efforts to kill the Great Satan.

The growth sectors of the United States economy have reaped enormous rewards from international marketing. Even some segments of traditional manufacturing have recovered by targeting specialty products, in steel, for example. But both have been joined and surpassed by iconic American exports such as fast food and sophomoric movies about men trapped in adolescence.

An American manifesto for the United States in the

twenty-first century that bases our current policies and practices on our founding beliefs is possible even in this era of historic change.

To guide our conduct at home, that manifesto will include the conviction that we are a commonwealth of all the people in which public institutions and resources are managed and protected in the common interest. It will insist that citizens have duties to protect their rights by participating in the public life of the nation in more than minimal and routine ways. That manifesto will include a demand that our government be committed to the national interest, an identifiable good greater than the sum of all the nation's special, personal, and private interests. And it will insist that public integrity be restored to government by restrictions on the ability of special interests to finance political campaigns through lobbyist contributions that guarantee special access to legislative and executive offices.

A manifesto for American conduct in the world of the twenty-first century can and should be rooted in our fundamental founding principles even, or perhaps particularly, in an age of great change. We seek good relations with all people of goodwill throughout the world. Even as we seek good relations, we wish to be free of foreign interference in our lives and affairs, and likewise commit to staying aloof from the internal affairs of other nations, including interception of their public and private communications. We do not intend to bring force to bear on those with whom we may disagree, and we do not expect them to bring force to bear on us. Our military forces are for our own protection, not to intimidate those with whom we disagree. If attacked, however, we will be intrepid in our location and persecution of those responsible. Do not tread on us and we will not tread on you. And we seek no empire whether political or economic but intend to engage constructively in the new international markets to everyone's mutual benefit.

An argument for restoring principle over expediency does not advocate for U.S. retreat from the world or for the abdication of responsibility. It advocates for less reliance on force, duplicity, and hypocrisy and more reliance on skillful diplomacy, common interests, and threat reduction. Our leadership is more effective and long-lasting when it comports with who we claim to be and what we claim to believe.

Within the boundaries of these enduring principles, it is possible to suggest an international leadership role based on the notion of a global commons.

The answer we give to three questions will largely determine whether the United States will flourish or decline in the twenty-first century. First: Will we anticipate events or merely react to them? Second: Will we form new alliances to address new realities? Third: How rapidly will we adapt to transformational change?

These questions share an assumption that the world is changing and changing fast. Our national predisposition, however, has been to rely on traditional institutions and policies, and use them to address unfolding history on our own timetable.

We are also inclined to employ a simple, all-encompassing, central organizing principle as a substitute for a national strategy. Unfortunately, the largely peaceful and prosperous 1990s were not used to develop a comprehensive strategic approach to an almost totally different new century that was emerging.

One lone effort represents the exception. In January 2001 the U.S. Commission on National Security for the Twenty-First Century produced a road map for national security for the first quarter of this century. It was almost totally ignored and only one of its fifty specific recommendations has been adopted a decade later, the creation of a Department of Homeland Security. It was as close to a comprehensive security, foreign policy, and domestic strategy as our nation produced at the turn of the century.

There are reasons for our lassitude, our false sense of security, and our reliance on reaction. Between 1812 and 2001, our continental home was not attacked. And because we are a large island nation, we have felt ourselves to be invulnerable.

Our economic expansion between the end of World War II and the first oil embargo of 1974 created a very large, productive, and secure middle class. We have possessed economic and military superiority for more than a half century.

And for most of our history, strategic thinking and planning, especially on the grand scale, have been enterprises confined largely to the academy. Instead, our policy makers dealt with events as they arose. Further, as a dominant power in the nation-state era, we could always try to rely on protectionism and tightened borders to keep the turbulent world at bay.

No longer. Isolation and a policy of reaction are impossible in the twenty-first century.

Multiple revolutions will continue to remake the world for decades to come. Globalization is making national boundaries economically redundant. Notice the mounting unresolved struggles within the Eurozone.

Further, information has replaced manufacturing as the economic base of our nation, and it is furiously integrating global networks. Together, globalization and information are eroding the sovereignty of nation-states, especially their monopolies on information and violence. And this erosion has contributed to the transformation of war and the changing nature of conflict. As the Arab Spring has demonstrated, the state no longer possesses the ability to control the free flow of information or has a monopoly on violence.

A world accustomed to a two-dimensional chessboard suddenly found that a third dimension had crystalized. Our nation had organized its international relations on the plane of the nation-state. In a heartbeat we are now forced to recognize the new dimension represented by the stateless nation.

It might be argued that this new reality dictates a wholly pragmatic, case-by-case response. It might better be argued, however, that now more than ever the United States requires a grand strategy that seeks to consistently apply its powers and resources to the achievement of its larger purposes over time, which was the definition of grand strategy provided by Basil Liddell Hart following World War I.

A new grand strategy is required because the new realities share two qualities. First, they cannot be adequately addressed by military means, and, second, they cannot be solved by one nation alone.

In addition, as events accelerate, response times shorten. Once a threat is immediate, deliberating, forming ad hoc responses and coalitions, and sifting through alternatives all become luxuries. In this century events and their repercussions will not wait for us to organize ourselves and our allies. A strategy of ad hoc reaction will not work.

This being true, deduction alone dictates a strategy that is internationalist, one that appeals to the common interests of the like-minded—that is to say, democratic—nations, one that anticipates and one that requires burden-sharing among those who occupy a global commons.

For it is the notion of a *global commons*, both actual and virtual, that should characterize America's twenty-first-century grand strategy. National goals now can be achieved *only* through increased international integration and collaboration.

Two powerful magnets are pulling the nations of the world together. One is globalization and the other is the ability to find out almost anything anywhere in the world virtually instantaneously. These forces have brought more people closer together than at any time in the history of mankind.

World leaders talk to each other by secure telephone at all hours of the day or night. Misunderstandings that caused world wars in previous centuries can be clarified in minutes. World organizations stabilize currencies, finance major projects, establish international communications standards, regularize international air-travel control, negotiate complex multilateral trade agreements, monitor maritime transportation, seek to establish environmental standards, pursue criminal syndicates, impose sanctions for aggression, quarantine pandemics, provide relief from natural disasters, and provide peacekeepers to separate belligerents. All these factors together provide a stability, if not necessarily a harmony, greater than at any time in human history. Taken together, all these forces provide a solid and unprecedented foundation for what American political leaders, behind closed doors, call a "new world order."

But so far they have not reacted to this change.

Even as these powerful integrating forces are imposing many layers of order on historically chaotic nationalistic systems, other forces, in some cases even more powerful ones, are breaking down traditional institutions and systems that provided a semblance of order.

A world order of empire and colonialism disintegrated during two world wars. As colonial powers surrendered their empires in Africa, Asia, and the Middle East, they either abandoned formerly occupied territories to the tribes and clans they had subdued or, as in the Middle East, drew arbitrary boundaries and imposed friendly despots to maintain order as well as guarantee oil supplies.

Following World War II, the Cold War created a bipolar world dominated by a United States–led North Atlantic Alliance and a Soviet-led Warsaw Pact. The two powers kept dual lids on percolating ethnic nationalism, ancient tribalism, and radical fundamentalism that rose to the surface when the lids came off in 1991.

Since then, a large number of factors have been at work undermining the integrated world created by globalization and information. As nation-states disintegrated, people sought identity in traditional cultures, religions, and tribal structures. The political systems based on state sovereignty first guaranteed by great-power colonialism and then by bipolar ideological competition began to melt.

Two other disintegrating forces emerged. As one faction,

religion, or tribe gained superiority in any venue, those opposed either were driven out or chose to flee, thus setting off
massive south-north migrations in Europe and North America. Large numbers of people migrated into Western Europe
from Turkey and North Africa, and similar numbers migrated
into the United States from Latin America.

This disruption of traditional ethnic structures and cultural norms in turn has, in recent years, given way to the rise
of right-wing political leaders and parties in almost all Western democracies. This ubiquitous new right is riding the tide
of racial resentments, employment competition, and cultural
transformation to gain political leverage and influence.

As in many European countries, immigration policy in
America is in confusion and stalemate. Borders are becoming
more porous (as the U.S. Commission on National Security
for the Twenty-First Century warned in 2001). Mass migration joins globalization and information in eroding national
borders—and therefore national identities. Birth certificates,
driver's licenses, and passports provide documentation of
national identity but they do not provide a sense of patriotism
and devotion to a historical nation.

National identity is preserved best in unitary nations such
as Poland more than in nations composed of immigrants such
as the United States. Yet Polish workers are building houses
in Italy and repairing plumbing in England even as Mexican
workers, many undocumented, replace roofs and clean up

fast-food kitchens in the United States and send their earnings to their families in Mexico.

All of this suggests that a new way must be found in the early twenty-first century to support traditional national identity on one hand while capitalizing on global integrating forces on the other. The key is common interests and the model is the original New England town square or commons.

Many, if not most, early New England settlements were built around a commons that became the central location for town meetings. Originally created for the common grazing of cattle, the commons soon became the location of the meeting hall, then the city hall, then the county courthouse. The commons was the place where community interests were discussed and decisions of common concern were made. The commons also was the rallying center for the common defense in case of outside trouble or attack.

Three centuries later there is now a global commons, but instead of a physical place it is a virtual commons created as much as anything else by global networks of instant communication. The collective interests of the global commons are extensive: security from terrorism; peaceful trade and commerce; communications, transportation, and finance; public health and the prevention of viral pandemics; security of borders and regulation of immigration; prevention of climate destruction; control of weapons of mass destruction; stabilization of currencies and rates of exchange; suppression of drug cartels; technological cooperation on massive experiments (such as CERN); collaboration on space exploration; and many other similar interests.

The United Nations is the central forum for many of these issues, such as global health concerns, refugees, and nuclear inspections. Yet it lacks the critical authority necessary to create structures for the governance of the global commons. And the UN was created seventy years ago when systems of modern communication did not exist.

Protection of national sovereignty is compatible with a new system of collegial cooperation in the common interests of all. Collaboration with other nations on a host of matters of common concern can be done without the sacrifice of national decision making or governing authority. Cooperating nations in the global commons will, in fact, find their authority enhanced by networking with the security, health, and other systems of friendly cooperating governments. Technology, especially computer technology, now makes cooperative governance much more possible and effective than ever before.

Allied armies in World War II offer an analogy for the global commons. Each national army in the alliance maintained its identity, weaponry, and command structure. Joint and collective planning and coordination were carried out by senior commanders from all members of the alliance. Each individual national army, navy, and air force was given its objectives and these were coordinated with one another. Some friction, confusion, and misunderstandings occurred at the operational levels between and among military services of individual alliance nations. But this massive endeavor was carried off without the highly sophisticated communication systems of today.

The de facto structure of much of a global commons order is already in place and operating in many separate arenas. The proposal is to recognize, systematize, and manage these arenas more formally.

Recent events offer context. In September 2014, President Obama announced what amounted to a de facto war against a newly emerged radical Sunni group calling itself the Islamic State that occupied parts of Syria and Iraq. He could do so, however, only after he, Secretary of State John Kerry, and other senior officials spent weeks lobbying a panoply of Arab states in the region. In haste, a strategy of sorts was put forward in which the United States would attack Islamic State forces from the air and unspecified military units from unspecified Arab states would attack on the ground. An American general was put in command of the operation.

Most experts agree that, even if this works, the operation will take years. Discovering that the strategy is unworkable will take less time. For our purposes, however, the question for consideration is whether a regional peacekeeping force resembling this hastily organized coalition could have been formed even as the United States was drawing down and ultimately withdrawing its forces from Iraq.

As a result of the U.S. invasion of Iraq, one fact is crystal clear: We had reopened bitter historical divisions between Shiite and Sunni Muslims that had been repressed for two decades under the crushing hand of Saddam Hussein. Sponsors of the invasion of Iraq in 2002 and 2003 had not taken such a possibility into consideration, but even if they had, it is evident this would not have deterred them. In any case, we left behind a strongly pro-Shiite, anti-Sunni government in Baghdad, and even as we departed, radical sectarian divisions and violence were on the march. Members of a global commons peacekeeping force could have been organized to prevent this from becoming malignant and explosive.

Yet another example, this one in the immediate future, of how a global commons might function is in the last global frontier, the Arctic Circle, which is rapidly being transformed by global warming. Major new sea-lanes of maritime transportation are opening. Rich reserves of oil and gas are being discovered on the seabed. Climate change is altering the environment by melting vast glaciers. The potential for conflicting territorial claims leading to friction and confrontation are apparent.

There is an Arctic Council composed of Russia, Canada, the United States, and the Scandinavian nations, but its focus to date has been largely environmental and it has yet to demonstrate the capacity to arbitrate maritime transportation claims, energy-resource competition, and international security matters of considerable consequence. The United States can and should undertake to make the Arctic region a major challenge for the global commons where all nations with a stake in its future commit to the anticipation and resolution of the myriad of new issues the Arctic opening presents.

In the summer and fall of 2014 the deadly Ebola virus broke out in West Africa, killing thousands. The UN's World Health Organization was overwhelmed and incapable of quarantining the virus, containing its spread, treating its victims, and handling the dead. Once again, an international appeal went out for help in all these areas. Health services in the advanced world have been warning of such a disaster for years. Yet no crisis response and management capability was in place. The global commons envisioned here would have organized this capability in anticipation of, not in reaction to, this and future crises.

The concept of the global commons offers a new way to think of our planet and its governance in the twenty-first century. It does, however, require the three key elements of leadership: the ability to look over the horizon and anticipate events; the imagination to construct and propose new solutions to address new realities; and the ability to convince a majority of citizens to follow a new course in response to those new realities.

Three guiding principles might structure such a U.S. strategy: economic innovation, networked sovereignty, and integrated security.

First: The United States cannot play a constructive global leadership role in organizing the virtual global commons without a fundamentally restructured economy. Global diplomatic engagement and international security cannot be financed with borrowed money. Neither true security nor leadership can be founded on debt. The only way for the United States to reliably pay for its international engagement and its security is by the revenue it generates through its own creative economic activity.

For the time being, the United States will remain superior in economic, political, and military terms. But we can maintain our leadership position over time only through economic innovation and creativity. We cannot continue to finance our military establishment with its far-flung operations by borrowing money from the Chinese and future generations.

Though it is becoming a somewhat worn theme, it is nonetheless true: We must invest public funds and private capital in science and technology, our universities and laboratories, corporate research, and multiple facets of innovation both to drive our own economic expansion and to market our innovations to the world.

Through the realignment of fiscal incentives and disincentives, the United States must transform itself from a debtor, a consuming nation, to a creditor, a producing nation. Governments and peoples around the world will find an economically creative United States an attractive model to follow. That attraction ensures U.S. international leadership. That leadership can organize the security of the global commons.

Second: Founding America's role in the world on the notion of a global commons requires identifying common threats *before* they become toxic, and it means identifying common interests requiring common pursuits in advance of those threats.

The primary resistance to the notion of a global commons is located in the concept of national sovereignty. But, as NATO proved following World War II and throughout the Cold War, shared security is not a threat to national identities and notions of self-governance.

There are a number of illustrations of how the security of the commons might work.

First: The public health services of advanced nations can be networked through common databases and communications systems to identify and quarantine viral pandemics before they spread and to organize medical response teams and regional stockpiles of immunization agents to facilitate containment. The 2014 African Ebola virus crisis is only the most recent illustration of why such a network is necessary and where it might be needed.

Second: An international constabulary force can be

created, possibly under NATO auspices, to manage failing states and tribal conflicts while diplomats negotiate restructuring agreements. Rwanda, Darfur, and Kosovo in the past and Somalia, Sudan, and Libya today all suggest conflicts that could have been anticipated and might be managed with much less loss of life.

Third: The existing International Atomic Energy Agency could be strengthened to become the indispensable agency for inspection of suspected manufacturing and stockpiling of weapons of mass destruction. Its mandate should be enforced and expanded, as it was not in Iraq, by the U.S. and the international community.

Fourth: It is not too soon to design an administrative and enforcement mechanism for an international treaty on carbon reduction; a climate treaty will not be self-enforcing.

Fifth: The most unstable region of the world, the Persian Gulf, is the source of a quarter of U.S. oil imports and a substantial amount of the importing world's supplies. Currently, the U.S. is the de facto guarantor of those oil supplies as well as the the policeman of the area's sea-lanes. Just as a loose consortium of nations with shipping interests now seeks to control piracy off the Somali coast, so a more tightly knit consortium should share responsibility for policing the Persian Gulf and guaranteeing all importing nations' oil supplies.

All these issues, and many more, represent the world of the

twenty-first century, much more a global commons than a hodgepodge of fractious nations and percolating conflicts in constant tension. Stable nations will increasingly find common cause in reducing and, where possible, eliminating local conflicts—through threat reduction and confinement—*before* they mutate and become toxic.

The central principle at work here is *networked sovereignty*, the willingness of participating nations to link their governing agencies and institutions with those of other friendly nations.

Nations, especially powerful nations, will continue to arm themselves. But they will find it appealing, politically and financially, to network their military assets in pursuit of common security interests. As NATO represents the triumph of collective security in a Cold War century, so new realities now require new alliances beyond the capabilities and mandate that NATO represents.

Forming new alliances with emerging regional power centers offers several advantages. Regional powers—China, India, Russia—should be made responsible partners rather than antagonists or rivals. Identifying mutual and collective security interests with the U.S. and formalizing a collective approach to securing these interests empowers regional leaders further and signals that the U.S. respects their legitimate concerns. Formal regional security alliances create diplomatic and administrative structures that anticipate, rather than react to, new realities and threats in their respective regions.

Thus, a third pillar of America's twenty-first-century strategy is integrated security. While a creative economy provides the resources, we pursue our global security in and through the global commons that we lead. A strong consortium of twenty to thirty nations can anticipate and minimize regional threats and can confine local conflicts before they become viral.

Nations not sharing democratic principles and institutions will find it profitable to begin to adopt these principles and institutions as the price of shelter under the security umbrella of the global commons. Political accommodation to enter the commons will more than pay for itself in enhanced shared security, including protection from pandemics, control of dangerous weapons, climate stabilization, isolation of terrorism, guaranteed oil supplies, and the stabilization of disintegrating states.

For example, there is every reason to create what might be called a *zone of international interest* in the Persian Gulf whereby a collection of major oil-importing nations guarantees continued distribution of petroleum resources from the region regardless of almost inevitable instability within and among the producing states. There are many reasons for having an international rapid-deployment force to intervene in failing states both to prevent civil wars and, if necessary, to create a security environment in which diplomats can manage a peaceful restructuring of nations.

Likewise, if climate damage creates massive dislocations due to increased coastal water levels, decreased water supplies, and crop dislocations, as predicted by senior retired military officers, the United States should now take leadership to create international institutions and capabilities to anticipate and limit the massive disruptions and destabilization these conditions will create.

Within the context of organizing the global commons as a diplomatic platform and security establishment, the United States will find it necessary to make several unilateral adjustments to its security policy to account for the new realities of the twenty-first century. The United States is an island nation, not a continental power. As such, we will require greater maritime assets, both for increased open-ocean operations as well as closer-to-shore conflict resolution and rapid-insertion operations.

To achieve these and other security objectives, however, we must acknowledge the political limits represented by organizing our security operations on an outdated statutory base. The National Security Act of 1947 has served us well for sixty-eight years, with some notable exceptions.

But, as Thomas Jefferson famously wrote, to expect each generation to govern itself with the laws and policies of previous generations is to expect a man to perpetually wear the coat he wore as a lad. Times change, and laws and policies, as well as institutions and the human mind, must keep pace.

Pakistan, whose instability imperils regional and possibly global security, is threatened by indigenous religious fundamentalists. Mexico is endangered by indigenous drug cartels that are de facto private armies. Iraq's and Afghanistan's ancient tribal and sectarian conflicts will continue for decades. Our massive military superiority cannot resolve these and a number of other conflicts by its sheer size and power.

Extended discussion on future security within the broader security community and public at large should encompass at least these questions:

What is the nature of the threats we face?

Which of these require military response and which do not?

Is the intelligence community properly coordinated and focused on emerging realities?

For nonmilitary concerns—such as failed states, radical fundamentalism, pandemics, climate degradation, energy dependence, and resource competition—are new international coalitions needed?

> Most of all, does our government require new
> legislative authority to achieve national security
> under dramatically changing conditions?

All these considerations and more should lead us to debate and adopt a new National Security Act for the twenty-first century. Oddly enough, no discussion of this necessity is taking place.

The net result of the comprehensive undertaking proposed here will be a twenty-first-century grand strategy for the United States, underwritten by a new statutory base that matches our economic, political, and military powers to the achievement of the larger purposes embodied in our continued international leadership. The principal product of this strategy will be the establishment of a twenty-first-century global commons to provide stability to the international community in this turbulent new century.

CONCLUDING THOUGHTS

Who are we as a nation? Are we still who our founders set us out to be? Or do the woes produced by world leadership for more than half a century inevitably require us to be a different nation?

The discipline of history should require a nation such as ours, one founded in principle but tempered by power, to periodically reassess our location, check our bearings, and recalibrate our national compass. This exercise would be timely after the end of a four-and-a-half-decade Cold War and the murky outcome of the two prolonged wars that followed. It is not so much an exercise in what we have learned as it is in assessing who we have become.

This suggestion is produced by a peculiarly American predilection toward self-analysis. If so, it is because America has always claimed more for itself than most other nations throughout history. We have believed ourselves to be different, if not also better, to have more noble ideals and more unselfish purposes. What other nation routinely asks for God's blessing on some occasions with the feeling that it is also our due.

But the nobler the ideals, the more scrutinized the performance.

Indisputably, after the allied success in World War II, the United States should not have retreated to its shores, though in that period there were many who believed we should have. Maintaining military bases in Europe and Asia, creating the United Nations and the Marshall Plan, and rebuilding Japan were politically controversial at home. President Truman spent immense amounts of political capital in convincing a majority of Americans of our nation's new role as world leader. In large measure he was successful because of increasing concerns about European weakness in frustrating Communist advances in Greece and other nations.

But maintaining more than two million Americans under arms was a substantial departure from the nation envisioned by our founders. Virtually overnight, our view of our security bounded by two oceans and two friendly neighbors gave way to a view that threats abounded in all parts of the world and we would neglect them at our peril.

Nothing symbolized this new security view more than the advent of intercontinental ballistic missiles carrying nuclear warheads. To retreat behind our traditional security boundaries was to invite nuclear blackmail in Europe, Asia, and elsewhere. Just as President James Monroe had advised European powers to leave their hands off the Western Hemisphere, now Truman and successive presidents told the Soviet Union to leave its hands off Europe and virtually everywhere else the United States now found new "national security interests."

While the United States economy grew at historic rates from the end of World War II until the mid-1970s, the financial costs of this global military deployment (some might say empire) were manageable. But circumstances changed with the formation of the Organization of the Petroleum Exporting Countries (OPEC) in 1960 and its initial effective embargo in

1974. Together with globalization and the rise of economic competition from Germany, Japan, and other former enemies and allies, the sharp rise in energy prices for the U.S.'s petroleum-based economy brought the growth of wealth to a standstill and created an economic plateau that we have been able to surmount only with technology and housing bubbles.

More troubling, however, was the rise of the security and surveillance state, including in the United States, where perceived security requirements clashed with Constitutional guarantees. Constitutional and legal rights of Americans were violated with the excesses of Watergate during the Nixon administration, which initially justified its violation of those rights on national security grounds—we needed to know whether those antiwar and civil rights groups were really Communist inspired—until it became clear that vulgar politics was the real reason. Thereafter, the megalithic surveillance "community" found it inconvenient or even impossible to separate surveillance of perceived terrorists from intrusion into the communications of everyday Americans who had been taught they were protected from their own government by the Constitution.

Throughout the complex seven decades since World War II, the majority of Americans have accepted the needs of the security and surveillance state to protect them from Communism and then terrorism. But our purposes here are to determine whether the price we have paid for security includes an erosion of our founding principles. If so, there are two choices: Either we insist that our leaders and their policies conform as closely as possible to the kind of nation we were meant to be and the nation we consider ourselves to be in our idealistic moments, or we accept that the world of the late twentieth and early twenty-first centuries requires the kind of pragmatism incompatible with those founding principles and therefore requires us to be less lofty in our presentation of ourselves to the world as an exceptional nation.

Proclamations of American exceptionalism have always been grating to leaders around the world, many of whom have seen serious departures from that proclaimed exceptionalism firsthand. But many everyday citizens around the world still see America in the twenty-first century as an international statue of liberty, a haven for those seeking a better life, and, most important, an embodiment of the practices of liberty and freedom to which almost all of mankind aspires.

We live in a time of instant global information. It is becoming increasingly untenable for the United States to speak one way and act another. The gap between principle and practice is now immediately evident. This reality may now have brought us to a historic point of departure: lay our claims of exceptionalism to rest or restore our principles and ideals as the basis for our actions at home and abroad.

Restoration of a Republic of Conscience and Principle is not incompatible with international leadership on a variety of fronts, from trade to foreign policy to security networks. Indeed, an America that leads by principle increases its strength and appeal. It adds a dimension of moral authority that has too often been missing in recent decades. For a Republic of Conscience, that is our greatest strength.

REFLECTIONS AND AFTERWORDS

Democratic republicanism, the faith of our fathers, is an inclusive approach (democratic) to government of and by the people (republican). In theory, it comes as close as humans can come to sustainable self-government. In practice in the United States, it is far from perfect. But as Winston Churchill said: "Democracy is the worst form of government, except for all the others that have been tried."

For those of us burdened with a remorseless sense of civic duty—still best summarized as "Ask what you can do for your country"—the struggle to create a more perfect union is never ending. There will never be a perfect union. Nevertheless, we must try to make it better. Thus, the label "progressive." It is a matter of promoting progress, often one step forward, then, too often, two steps back.

For some, this pursuit takes the form of a civic religion in which politics (with a small "p") takes place within a temple or, on great occasions, a cathedral. That temple of democracy and republicanism is sacred in a secular sense. When tainted by money changers, as it is today on a massive scale, there is a duty to drive the money changers out. When the elders of this civic religion, in this case the Supreme Court of the United States, endorse the money changers, the task becomes that much more difficult.

The story of how a young small-town Kansas boy joined this civic religion is instructive. There was an eighth-grade public school class called Civics. The Constitution was the Bible. The Declaration of Independence was a creedal statement. The writings of the early Founding Fathers a testament to their purposes. Being a literalist at heart, that boy took it all very seriously. Here was something to believe in—one's country, the United States of America—that provided purpose and foundation during the days between Sundays.

Aside from voting when one came of age, what did recruitment into this civic religion entail? Words such as "participation" and "involvement" and "paying attention" were tossed about without a great deal of clarity. Then a dawn of sorts occurred in my late college years. A new young presidential candidate, totally different from the rotund, backslapping, cigar-smoking political stereotype, issued a challenge that seemed directly addressed to me and my generation. Public service is a duty. You must protect your rights by performing your citizen duties. The message resonated.

That message was as old as democracy itself. As later study revealed, it came from ancient Athens and progressed through the Roman Republic and then, like a hidden cult, mysteriously appeared and reappeared in small republics sporadically before and after the Dark Ages and provided insight and energy to the Scottish and English Enlightenment. And that Enlightenment provided the intellectual foundation for the principles underlying the democratic republic of our founders.

With varying degrees of intensity—for Jefferson higher, for Hamilton lower—those founders believed, proclaimed, and wrote that the large-scale republic they were creating would survive "for our posterity" only if citizens did their duty, and their duty was to preserve and protect their faith in that civic religion and to seek to make it "more perfect."

If the winds of change require a principled republic to adapt to new realities, it must do so with due regard for those principles upon which it was founded. Thus the United States had little recourse but to remain in Europe and Asia following World War II despite early warnings against foreign entanglements. To withdraw to Fortress America was to invite destabilizing conflicts that would almost inevitably have led to yet a third major expeditionary war in the twentieth century.

But accepting that burden did not require recourse to unprincipled behavior involving everything from overthrowing governments to assassinating foreign leaders. A worldwide network to collect information and process it until it became intelligence did not require clandestine operations in the back alleys of the world. Not every local or regional conflict required U.S. military intervention to demonstrate our strength. And no terrorist threat thus far has justified the wholesale surveillance of communications between Americans and the violation of their rights to privacy.

Our founders were wise enough to know that our emerging nation, even one that adopted doctrines such as manifest destiny, would be engaged (though not entangled) in the world. They would, however, have condemned the excesses to which that engagement has led us.

Even more disturbing to the founders of our civic religion, however, would be the sinister and corrupting network of lobbying, campaign financing, and special interest access to policy makers and legislators that now forms a cancer on our democratic republic. And even more troubling to America's founders would be the complete loss of disinterestedness—government officials who have no personal stake in their decisions—as represented by the hundreds of former administration officials and members of Congress now filling the lobbying battalions.

They would have seen years ago this danger to our Republic that those without any sense of civic duty might seek a seat in Congress with the express intent of leaving after a term or two to barter for a seat at the high-stakes Casino on the Potomac that their government had become.

It is staggering to contemplate that a self-proclaimed "originalist" justice on the United States Supreme Court could seriously believe our founders would have concluded that an artificial legal construct like a corporation had the same First Amendment right of free speech as individual Americans and, therefore, could invest as heavily as it chose in electing officials favorable to its financial interests. Such a senior member of the judicial branch could not have read a word of Jefferson or James Madison. So much for "originalism."

Stock markets may boom. Trade may increase. Our economy may rebound. Deficits may even be reduced. But these are sad and perilous times in the temple of democratic republicanism. The great ship of state has slipped its moorings, moorings in principles of civic duty, justice, equality, and integrity in government.

There is a disquiet in the land that income and wealth alone will not resolve. "What doth it profit a man if he gain the whole world and lose his soul?" Our nation has a soul, I believe. The quantifying categories of political science will never find it. The armies of money changers in the temple of government would not recognize it. Those committed to careers in elective office too often have to barter their souls to achieve that purpose. Those who manipulate wealth in the financial corridors on Wall Street are more concerned with interest rates than intangibles such as souls. Ideologues occupying the political extremes are more concerned with rigid adherence to the purity of their dogmas than with preserving our nation's soul.

In describing the duties of one generation to the next and to the future, past leaders have often relied on the image of the torch. We receive that torch from our parents and pass it to our children with the hope they will do likewise. We each must ask ourselves how well we have done in keeping the torch aflame, in keeping our ideals, as tattered as the vicissitudes of life have made them, alive. Young people, in that age when ideals burn brightest, often look for that torch, for national direction, for purpose and meaning.

Sadly, that torch is not burning as brightly as it should these days. Ego and self-interest are dominant and, in all but a few cases, overwhelm the nobility of public service. Leaders asking what we can do for our country would be trampled if they placed themselves between new graduates and Wall Street.

There are heroes. They are engaged in feeding the hungry and educating the poor. They are young Foreign Service officers going off to remote countries. They are housing the homeless and teaching their children to read. They are getting inner-city young people to engage in community service in exchange for educational opportunities.

We hear too little of them from media obsessed with scandal and human error. These heroes are "making a difference," but news of their actions is too often buried amid a hailstorm of stories about misconduct and misdeeds. But they represent a humanitarian strain in the American character, particularly among the young, that not every nation can replicate. That inclination must be restored to public office and public service if our quest to reclaim our founding heritage is to succeed.

We do not live in an age of idealism. Perhaps such an age can never be recaptured. But we should try. Our leaders should once again ask what we can do for our country rather than easily slip into the cynical political advisor's direction to demonize "Washington." How is it possible to claim to love this country and hate its government? But that has become the default position of the permanent political class.

Being one of the diminishing number of survivors of that more idealist generation of almost a half century ago is to be tempted toward nostalgia. Except that recapturing some of that sense of public service and national progress is necessary if we are to come even close to the restoration of our Republic and its principles.

Are our current leaders that much more worldly, sophisticated, and skeptical than John F. Kennedy was in his day and therefore incapable of appealing to the idealism of youth? Or are they afraid of ridicule in an age when skepticism is slipping quickly into cynicism? If "Washington" is as disreputable and ineffective as they claim it to be, then it is awkward to urge young people to engage in public service in that government.

It is tempting to conclude that early twenty-first-century American politics and government are in a cul-de-sac from which they are incapable of emerging. There are few political heroes. There are even fewer statesmen and stateswomen.

Statesmen of both genders know political intricacies but refuse to be limited by them. They use experience, knowledge of history, keen judgment, and wisdom to further their nation's interest. They know the art of negotiation but seldom cut corners or compromise principles. They demonstrate integrity and character to prevent bringing dishonor to the nation they serve.

Perhaps more than any other quality defining a statesman is that of a sense of history. Ignorance of history precludes perspective. "Those who cannot remember the past are doomed to repeat it" is usually attributed to George Santayana. Harry Truman's version was "The only new thing in the world is the history you do not know." And, in the House of Commons in 1935, Winston Churchill observed that "it falls into that long, dismal catalogue of the fruitlessness of experience and the confirmed unteachability of mankind. Want of foresight, unwillingness to act when action would be simple and effective, lack of clear thinking, confusion of counsel until the emergency comes, until self-preservation strikes its jarring gong—these are the features which constitute the endless repetition of history."

All this is brought to mind by recalling the events of World War I in the Middle East that produced the political chickens now coming to roost a hundred years later. It is a tragic history of late colonial overreach by Britain and France, the worst kind of treachery, deceit, and diplomatic betrayal, and fateful political decisions based on misinformation, wishful thinking, and an almost total ignorance of Arab culture and history.

The results now rest on America's doorstep, a nation late to enter the World War I jungle of old nineteenth-century European intrigue and guided only by a dreamy Wilsonian idealistic hope for the end of bloodshed and a liberated world safe for democracy. Even as they were secretly carving up the Middle East, Wilson's British and French allies scoffed at his naïveté.

It says much that one of the few Americans on the scene in Cairo and elsewhere during this period was a young employee of the Standard Oil Company named William Yale who was taken on board as an advisor to the secretary of state simply because he had spent time in the region locking up oil concessions for his company. This was a predictor of the future of U.S. interests in the Middle East if there ever was one.

From 1941 onward, U.S. policy in the region was to keep Arabian, Persian, and Iraqi oil out of the hands of the Nazis and then the Soviets. It was, after all, *our oil.* We overthrew a democratic prime minister of Iran according to that logic and guess what that got us? U.S. policy toward Saudi Arabia has been dominated by oil. And we should not think for a minute that the invasion of Iraq wasn't guided in major part by access to oil reserves, though the clever invasion plotters somehow never found it convenient to admit it. (Their charade went like this: "Oil? Gee whiz, is there oil there?")

"All that is history" is the casual way of dismissing uncomfortable truths, that is, until those truths come back to haunt us. It is a pity George W. Bush had not studied more history. But the lessons of history are best learned before, not after, becoming president.

Why did Santayana say "cannot" instead of "will not"? Will not is a failure of choice. Cannot is a failure of ability. Are Americans incapable of learning history? If so, our nation's future will not be a pretty one. A mark of statesmanship is the ability to learn from history and apply its lessons to current conflicts and skillful avoidance of future crises. But genuine statesmanship is in short supply. It might help future statesmen if former diplomats, including past secretaries of state, included lessons learned in their respective memoirs.

In part, we cannot learn from history because we are a pragmatic people. We make it up as we go along. Each new day offers a new experience and a new chance to try something different. It is refreshing, but it is also innocent and childlike. But there is little that is truly new and different, and the circularity of human experience gives fate the opportunity to come back and bite us.

Had we known Vietnamese history, we would have known the guiding principle to its conflict was nationalism, not Communist ideology. Had we known Iranian history, we would have known the people wanted self-determination, not an oligarchical shah. Had we known Russian history, we would have known the critical importance of Crimea's ports to

Russia's access to the sea. Had we known Middle Eastern history, we would have known the deep territorial and theological divide between Sunni and Shia that has existed for more than thirteen centuries.

Our experience with the CIA in Iran in the 1950s offers instruction in what goes around comes around. It is always tempting to write about repeating the mistakes of the past by not learning from them. The temptation arises from the fact that this is so true and occurs so often in U.S. foreign policy. Since the disappearance of the Soviet Union and the Cold War, a movement usually called neoconservatism has specialized in promoting doctrines of interventionism, imposing democracy on complex foreign venues, demonstrating American "strength" (always military) as a means of frightening opponents, and defining American exceptionalism always in bellicose terms.

All this was brought to mind by the book *Patriot of Persia* by Christopher de Bellaigue, which chronicles the CIA-conducted 1953 overthrow of Muhammad Mossadegh, a reformist Iranian prime minister. Mossadegh represented Iran's first chance to move toward something like a Turkish-style parliamentary democracy. We joined the British in overthrowing him because he nationalized the Anglo-Iranian oil company. In those days and thereafter, anyone who would do such a thing was thought to be a Communist. This all occurred during a period when the United States went about overthrowing governments in a number of countries simply because they refused to line up on our side early in the Cold War. In almost every case we imposed a U.S.-friendly dictator on the country and supported him with troops and dollars. Power became a substitute for democratic principle.

In the Iranian case, our leader of choice was a shah from the largely self-described princely Pahlavi family, and he controlled things for the next quarter century through a notoriously ruthless secret police force called the SAVAK. He was overthrown in 1979, not by Communists but by equally ruthless fundamentalist Muslim mullahs who shortly thereafter took all the inhabitants of the U.S. embassy in Tehran hostage for the next year and a half. Except for the colorful and bizarre effort during the Reagan administration to sell Israeli weapons to the Iranians to raise money to conduct covert "contra" wars in Central America (all to bypass Congress and the laws of the U.S.), that has pretty much brought us to where we are today.

The law of unintended consequences is at work here in a big way. The neoconservatives who now advocate extensive bombing of and war with Iran could not be bothered to connect the dots of history that led back to the overthrow of Mossadegh and brought us today's Iran.

When was the last time anyone could remember a serious debate in the U.S. Senate, let alone one that featured references to the lessons of history? To understand history, one must first read it. If senators today are reading and understanding history, they are concealing the evidence of doing so.

That may be understandable. There are few votes to be had by reminding Americans of the follies and mistakes of our past, especially if you are one who voted for them.

Eventually, British duplicity undid the Arab revolt and denied Arab ambitions for self-determination in the region. But T. E. Lawrence had studied Arabic and Arab history before riding his camel into the desert and eventually helping to kindle a semblance of unity among disparate Arab tribes to overthrow Ottoman domination and inspire Arab hopes. Based on his studies of history, he believed and helped inspire the Arab dream. But what could he know? He was only twenty-nine years old when his nation's senior statesmen and politicians betrayed him and the Arabs, and left us with the bitter outcome a century later.

There are so few statesmen because too many politicians sacrifice honor in the pursuit of short-term gain or in the pursuit of a politically dictated policy that soon proves to be flawed. There is a simple test of integrity: When was the last time a statesmen or senior government figure resigned rather than promote a dubious or flawed policy? Secretary of State Cyrus Vance did so out of opposition to a failed hostage rescue mission in Iran in 1980. There have been few if any such resignations since. From this, it is difficult not to conclude that principle is routinely sacrificed in the hope of retaining high office or presidential favor.

There are trends and tides in human affairs that come and

go. Few things are inevitable in history. Though resistance is strong, there is nothing to prevent this great nation from recapturing its founding ideals and principles. But will it take a serious economic decline, a depression, or a large-scale recession—or, even worse, an international crisis—that is genuinely threatening our security to cause us to once again become the nation we were meant to be? Those who fought in World War II and those who supported those who fought have been called the Greatest Generation. But there have been other generations from our founding through our terrible civil war to the Great Depression that were great as well. It is unfortunate that crisis and threats to survival seem required to bring out the best in our nation.

Let us hope that serious danger is not required to create national unity. By that time, it could be too late. And that serious danger might not be a nuclear attack; it might be a highly contagious virus. Our hope is that we can recapture some sense of national unity—community, shared interest, patriotism, or whatever it may be called. Despite vague hopes for a man, or woman, on a white horse to lead us forward, there is little if any chance of this happening, if for no other reason than our Constitution is set up to make such a figure virtually impossible. Our founders were afraid of only a few things. But men on white horses were one of them. Their European fathers had seen enough of those and history offered few positive examples.

If there is a shortcut to the hard work of citizen duty, it is not self-evident. Oscar Wilde once buried socialism with three words: "Too many evenings." That comes uncomfortably close to what it means to be the citizen of a republic. One or two evenings from time to time are not too much to ask. Remember the Norman Rockwell painting *Freedom of Speech* that portrays an everyday working American standing up and speaking at a town meeting? That's what being the citizen of a republic means. He is not only free to speak, he also has a duty to speak.

Thomas Jefferson believed that public education was central to the flourishing, if not also the survival, of the American Republic. He wanted to ensure that when everyday citizens attend and speak at town hall meetings, they know what they are talking about—in contrast, for example, with the recent notorious demand to "keep your dirty government hands off my Medicare." This is the difference between a right—free speech—and a duty—make sure your speech is based on facts and is not a recycled partisan talk-show rant.

Despite the fervent hopes of some extreme anarchist elements, the government of the United States is not going away. Nor is it going to be reduced to the Department of Defense and the Federal Bureau of Investigation. There are highways and dams to be built and rebuilt, there are schools to be built and teachers to be paid, there are research laboratories curing diseases and launching new scientific discoveries that must be supported, and, yes, there are elderly and poor Americans who need our help.

Taxes are the price we pay for a civilized society, and these and other necessary public functions do not produce profits, at least in the short term, and thus are of little if any interest to corporations and private investors. There is, however, a very long list of government projects, from jet engines to nuclear reactors, that eventually became giant private industries producing tens of thousands of jobs and very large profits.

When the glue that holds society together dries and cracks, people suffer. Elderly people who do not have children in local public schools are too often opposed to even minimal property tax increases for school repairs and teachers' salaries. Too many people who have private recreational opportunities and who rarely if ever visit national parks and wilderness areas believe these public resources should be privatized for corporate development and profit. The interests of future generations are forgotten or dismissed. Those wealthy few on whom fortune has smiled too often resist contributing to the medical care for the indigent elderly.

Despite the sound and fury over government, the real issue is more profound. Some time back, in an exercise in balancing our national budget, a friend and former Senate colleague said, "The issue is how much government we want." To which my response was, "The issue is what kind of society we want."

Government is but the instrument by which we guide and

direct our society and shape its priorities through national elections. The issue is not the size of government. The issue is the effectiveness of government. Making government effective is the burden of the executive branch and the duty of the administrator. Those philosophically opposed to government seldom are good at making it work. Indeed, they might have incentives to demonstrate its failures.

Somewhere, perhaps only in the imagination, there is a republic composed of those who have reached a more or less permanent consensus as to the purpose and function, and therefore size and shape, of our government. There would be a governing consensus between political parties and competing ideologies regarding budget priorities and divisive social issues. That government would be run by adults who knew how to talk to one another in civil tones and who put the public and national interest foremost. With varying results, our great nation has been searching for this very government for 230 years. It is not too wild a dream to imagine we can actually achieve it. It is difficult to see how we can achieve that government without, at the outset, first restoring the founding principles that formed our country.

Reconciling the practical problems of governing in an era of new twenty-first-century realities with the highly idealistic purpose of principled behavior is difficult, but it is not impossible. Indeed, America's political leadership might find itself surprised by the goodwill, possibly even greater cohesion, we might find among our existing and potential allies when we actually behave according to the principles we proclaim.

There is a considerable difference between dreamy idealism, which Woodrow Wilson was rightly or wrongly accused of on occasion, and a practical idealism that shapes its policies to fit its principles rather than the reverse.

This book is not simply about the evils of political prerogative and divisions between Court and Country. In a nation where wealth is increasingly rising to a narrow top and power is concentrated in a corrupted political system, powerful questions are raised about the future of the Republic (if a semblance of the original Republic remains). Will young men and women continue to volunteer to fight in dubious wars with unclear purposes and slim chances for success? Will future generations believe it worth their lives to protect an increasingly unjust and unfair political society, especially one that recognizes the symbols, such as the flag, but not the reality of their sacrifice? Will everyday Americans, seeing the systematic flight of corporate profits from a reasonable tax obligation, undertake to avoid their own obligation to pay for government services?

At some point, corruption of a republican system of government destroys not only the republican form of government but also the citizens' faith and confidence in that government. Erosion of citizen trust, already under way due to Watergate and the insider cronyism in Washington, accelerates as the unfairness and injustice of a governing system convinces citizens that the political and economic deck is stacked against them.

This is not a warning of an American collapse. It is a serious suggestion that we all clearly understand the consequences of the corruption of our system. Older democracies, less attentive to their history than we are to the unique character of the early American Republic, continue to function in some cases more fairly than do we. But, by and large, those older democracies do not hold themselves out to be the novel and historic departure in self-government that we do. In abandoning our republican heritage, we are risking the loss of our citizens' confidence in who we are as a nation.

There is a current lament regarding the perceived loss of U.S. leadership, though those responsible for the lament rarely if ever define how that leadership should be demonstrated. The unspoken definition of leadership is the use of military power. Currently, there is little appetite in the United States for yet another major military deployment. Since diplomacy is not a favorite arena for the confrontational, the vague appeal to leadership masks a more direct military proposal.

But all the military might in the world, and America's might is far greater than most others combined, will not create international followership among nations against whom we have mounted covert operations or in which we have carried out mass-communications intercepts or in which we have manipulated local politics. To align principle and practice in foreign relations, our leaders might profitably adopt the Golden Rule: Do unto others as we would have them do unto us. When our exceptionalism is genuine, it is incompatible with double standards.

Given our great fortune in geography, natural resources, and uncommonly inventive people, there is little reason for fearing an irreversible decline that would follow the pattern of the great nations of the past. We neither have nor seek empire, though we came perilously close in the Middle East with the invasion of Iraq. The threats we face, from terrorists armed with weapons of mass destruction to climate change to viral pandemics, are manageable and do not represent a so-called existential threat.

The issue is not our survival but rather what we survive to be. Great Britain lost an empire and still searches for a destiny. Russia survived the collapse of the Soviet Union but still persists in trying to regain its older Russian empire. China seeks hegemony in its coastal regions and free-range exploitation of African and Latin American resources but has its hands too full managing a billion and a half increasingly restless people to attempt global dominance. For those hawkish Americans who need a peer political and military competitor to justify large defense budgets, all this is a frustration.

The United States will move forward into the twenty-first century, but in what form? We have the choice to continue the

Cold War and post–Cold War practices of power politics and expediency adopted by the great powers of history, and if we do so, we will increasingly come to resemble them. No better, no worse. Or we can take the hard road, one that will restore our most cherished principles, which justify our claim to exceptionalism.

In recent times it seems as if almost every account of public service in the foreign policy arena involves hard choices. This suggests, perhaps unwittingly, that choices in times past were less difficult. Our founders might be sympathetic but hardly understanding. Their choices make those choices of today by an unchallenged superpower seem tame by comparison. And those decisions they didn't or couldn't resolve among themselves they left to truly historic leaders such as Abraham Lincoln. Current leaders should not invite a discussion of hard choices with the spirit of Abraham Lincoln.

On analysis, what makes the choices hard today is not that they often involve the better versus the best, but that they involve right and wrong. The central argument of this essay is that most so-called hard choices are between principle and expediency. Have former and present foreign policy administrators chosen to side with autocratic dictators who happened to be the enemy of our enemy at the price of compromising our democratic principles? Too often. Are there occasions where the betrayal of our principles has come back to haunt us? Again, too often.

America in the Cold War world and beyond has let short-term expediency replace longer-term principle too often. Because we knew it was wrong, more often than not our principles were left behind in the dark. We could deny overthrowing Iranian Prime Minister Muhammad Mossadegh to help the British protect their (and our) oil, and we made a bitter enemy of the Iranians. We could let the Central Intelligence Agency promote a partnership with the Mafia to assassinate Fidel Castro, but most of Latin America knew about it and we fostered a half-century stalemate with a tiny island in the Caribbean. We could reject early overtures by Ho Chi Minh for help in liberating a colonized Vietnam because we needed French support in the Cold War, and this cost 58,000 American lives.

Twenty-first-century American politics make it very difficult to avoid hypocrisy. The *New York Times* documents the recent trend by President Obama to concentrate power in the executive branch by issuing executive orders to achieve results against congressional opposition. My instantaneous reaction was: Good for him.

But then it is necessary to recall that this is exactly what George W. Bush did and many of us feared for the Constitutional system of checks and balances. The founders of the Republic feared concentrated power in the executive branch knowing throughout history that this—in addition to special interest corruption—was the surest way to destroy a republican form of government.

It is human nature to excuse behavior when the result is what we favor and to condemn that same behavior when the result is what we oppose. This is the pragmatic approach to politics, an approach much favored these days. But what about the violation of principle?

It is a matter of principle that too much power in the presidency, regardless of how it is used, is a threat to a balanced system of government. Precedents are established, and it is undeniable that the next Republican president will cite Obama's precedent for taking unilateral executive action to achieve his or her results, and progressive people will rise up to condemn it.

But there is a distinction between the Bush and the Obama precedents. George W. Bush, and the lawyers who advised him, claimed some kind of theory they called the "unitary executive," which means, in effect, that the president could do pretty much anything he wanted to do. To any student of republican government, that sounded like a claim of unlimited authority and a truly frightening proposition. To the degree the Obama administration has made any claim, it is simply that he faces an impenetrable opposition in the House and now a Republican-controlled Senate opposed to virtually every major legislative initiative and even second- and third-tier administrative appointments. There is a difference here, and it is a vitally significant one.

Nevertheless, it is necessary even for progressives and Obama supporters to understand the implications for history and the future of concentrated power in the White House. The day will surely come when that kind of authority will be used, even more than it has been already, to violate Fourth Amendment freedoms, to justify unconstitutional searches and seizures, to place citizens under surveillance, and to violate due process of law. And the justification will be one of expediency: We had no choice. We had to act.

Even as we nod in agreement when the president says, "We can't wait," we will find it necessary to think about how a future, less benign president will say the same thing to support reconstitution of the imperial presidency.

My experience is that no bad deed by our country goes unnoticed or unremembered. That experience also supports the conviction that when we act in secret, it is seldom to hide the act from our enemies and much more often an attempt to hide our leaders' behavior from the American people. When our leaders insist on reverting to "hard choices" as a plea for understanding and perhaps sympathy, they are almost always acknowledging, whether they realize it or not, how difficult it is to violate our national conscience in the interest of expediency.

Doing what is right is often difficult, but it almost never has to be explained. Honoring our nation's principles is self-evidently the right thing to do. It may be awkward in international diplomacy but it almost never requires justification. Behaving on principle in international affairs should never be a hard choice.

My conversion as a Constitutional evangelist quite probably occurred during the years of 1975 and '76 when I was a member of the Church Committee. This deep immersion in the dark rivers of covert operations was, for a young senator, a revelation and not a happy one. Reading the Cold War spy thrillers of the day was no preparation for the real world. We were waging the Cold War not by appeals to principles and ideals, nor by pledging allegiance to the Republic for which our flag stands, but by resorting to the least principled activities imaginable.

And it was clear that these operations were no secret to the people against whom they were directed. They were kept secret so the American people would not know (some said they did not want to know) what our government was doing in their name. The so-called secret bombing of Cambodia during the Vietnam War was no secret to the Cambodians who were being bombed. It was kept secret from the American people whose elected representatives had not authorized war on the Cambodians. Likewise, the massive surveillance of Americans carried out by the National Security Agency more recently was kept secret from all but a few members of Congress and thus from those of us placed under surveillance.

Twenty-first-century America did not simply deviate from its principles as an expedient to conduct the Cold War and then return to its principled base. The attacks of 9/11 gave new cause for the resumption and continuation of the practices of nations throughout history that have not made idealistic claims for themselves. This raises the highly troublesome possibility that we have now adopted a permanent course away from the nation we were created to be. When our leaders claim it is a hard choice between supporting friendly dictators and standing up for the rights of freedom-seeking people, we know we are well down that easy road of becoming just like everyone else.

Has it now become too late to preserve the Republic our founders created or is there still a chance to redeem a heritage distinct from other nations? It is not too late. But preserving our Republic well into its third century, and after decades of marginally principled behavior, will require leaders who understand the true hard choice is to pursue policies based on the timely renewal of our founding principles.

Ingrained in human nature is the desire to leave a legacy, usually defined in material terms, to our children. Those on whom fortune has smiled often amass estates of property and bank accounts that guarantee their children a comfortable future. Even in this nation of wealth, however, most of those estates are modest at best.

But even for those who amass great wealth, it is surprising

how little thought is given to the public legacy we all leave our children and future generations. The children of the wealthy may inherit millions of dollars, but if the air is dangerous to breathe and the water dangerous to drink, if climate temperatures continue to rise and coastal water levels rise with them, if one in five American children lives in poverty, if American troops continue to die in endless tribal wars, if our public schools decay, if our political process is even more corrupt, if we squander rather than conserve our finite natural resources, that will be the public legacy left to the children of great wealth.

They will, of course, have means of escape—private yachts and airplanes, private resorts, gated communities, private security forces to guard the gates, exclusive schools for their children, and endless isolation from the greater American community, society, and nation. Unless those concerned with amassing legacies of private wealth consider also the public legacy they leave their own posterity, and exercise the kind of civic virtue that our founders believed our Republic required to survive, they will not only leave behind an even more deeply divided America but also one that their heirs will seek to escape.

It is a mystery how parents who demonstrate every concern for the future well-being of their offspring in private terms can so blithely ignore the greater social and political national context those heirs also inherit. Deep in the souls of early American republican founders was the conviction that we had a moral obligation to leave behind a nation better than we found it, but one still solidly based on the timely renewal of the first principles that prevented the erosion by corruption of our Constitution.

That is the meaning of a Republic of Conscience. It exists somewhere above the political republic by which we govern ourselves. It is a realm of conviction, principle, ideals, and, yes, dreams of a more perfect union. It is what makes us try to participate in a political process that deflects principle at every turn and prevents us from giving up.

During ages of skepticism and cynicism, people of quality direct their energies toward humanitarian causes, feeding poor children through Share Our Strength, or educating low-income students through Citizen Schools, or providing community service through City Year, or combating disease through international health organizations. But the grit and determination these efforts require must be supported by a principled United States government that rises above the clutches of influence and accepts the genuine hard choice of principled behavior. Only then will we have a chance to provide our posterity with the public legacy it needs and deserves, and only then will we have fulfilled the mandate left to us by our founders. This will not be easy. But it must be done to recapture the Republic we were challenged to keep for our posterity, to renew the first principles of our Constitution, and to become once again a Republic of Conscience.

FINAL THOUGHTS

||||||||||||||||||||||||||||||||||||||||||||||||||||||||||||||||||||||||||

Why write a book like this? I wrote it for a very simple reason: I care about this country. I've cared about it all my long life and I still do. And I've done what any citizen who cares about his or her country does. I've tried to make it better.

The more I've thought about it—and I've thought about it a great deal—the more that care had to do with making America what it was intended to be. The founders had an idea that they were creating a government for a nation of potentially great wealth. Some of the more visionary of them contemplated great cities and westward expansion and a singular role in the world.

But the record they left behind, and it's an extensive one, has to do with the kind of government they believed the new America should have. And there is every evidence that they wanted, even expected, future generations to perpetuate that government. They even went so far as to say that if their government changed—by letting corruption destroy its republican character—this would no longer be the nation they intended to create.

They left us a legacy, one that could only be honored through the performance of our duties. Our duties as citizens are to nurture and protect the republic, to place the commonwealth—the national interest—above all the narrow and special interests, to resist concentrated wealth and power, to prevent privilege from residing in only a handful of families, to participate in the life and governance of America, and to hand to each succeeding generation a republic free of corruption and full of the lessons of these duties.

We have drifted far away from that legacy and the founders' mandate. Whether we have passed some political point of no return—the abandonment of the republican commonwealth—only history will record. I pray not.

This book is one citizen's testament, a testament to the political faith of our founders. It is an imperfect attempt to shine a light on a perfectly clear record made over a few months in late eighteenth-century America and to contrast that clear record with early twenty-first-century America. As a nation and a people we have changed because new realities required us to change and adapt. But have we become a different nation in the process? I pray not.

What a great opportunity the new generation of Americans has to restore our republican heritage and ideals. There can be no greater challenge and no greater opportunity. In the process, if even a few young Americans accept this challenge, they will restore to this country the spirit of idealism my generation felt a long half century ago.

As someone once said, it is because I am an idealist that I know I am an American.

ACKNOWLEDGMENTS

"Write about why we all feel so bad," she said. That was Philippa Brophy in mid-2014, "Flip" to all who know her and have benefited from her matchmaking in the interest of books over the years, matchmaking that helps book writers find book publishers. Such specialists are usually called agents in the publishing world, but the very few genuinely talented ones, like Flip, are much more—part psychoanalyst, part negotiator, and part alchemist. She certainly deserves credit for the core question this book seeks to answer.

Why do Americans, still enjoying a reasonably high standard of living, peace, and security, feel bad? The answer offered here has to do with a gap, a disparity, a distance between who we believe ourselves to be and who we have become.

Thanks to Flip's thorough knowledge of the book publishing world, she understood that one editor/publisher would know what I was talking about. And, in introducing me to David Rosenthal at Penguin Random House's Blue Rider Press, her matchmaking once again was highly perceptive.

David already had a feeling that America's deep discontent had roots in a vision lost, a mission betrayed, a promise abandoned. Our national disquiet is found in the distance between conscience and corruption, between country and court, between the national interest and an army of special interests, between principle and power. This is the story David Rosenthal wanted told and the story, based on a lifetime of experience, I have tried to tell.

David's colleagues at Blue Rider, including David Hough, Marie Finamore, and Aileen Boyle, deserve mention and praise for meticulous editing and tasteful promotion.

I have attempted to bring a lifetime of study in philosophy, religion, law, and political theory to bear in this meditation. But, more than any other factor, service in years gone by with United States senators of extraordinary wisdom, principle, conscience, and dedication to our nation's interests and the common good have strengthened my instincts and guided my convictions.

The United States was founded as a republic, a republic on a scale never before attempted. Like all republics throughout history, the American Republic is subject to destruction by corruption, and the republican ideal defines corruption as placing narrow or personal interests ahead of the interests of the commonwealth. The great senators with whom I served may or may not have been historians of the republic, but few if any joined the rising legions of lobbyists now occupying our nation's capitol.

I have studied the history and theory of the republic for many years and have benefited from the writings of many scholars. Two stand out: Professor Gordon Wood and Professor Joyce Appleby. I continue to learn by reading and rereading their keenly perceptive interpretations of our nation's founding.

I am grateful to Flip, David, and David's colleagues for enabling this argument to be made and to my former Senate colleagues for confirming my conviction of its merits. And, as always, Lee, Andrea, and John have enriched my life beyond expression.

A former United States senator and presidential candidate, Gary Hart is the author of twenty-one books, including his Oxford doctoral dissertation on Jefferson's ideal of the republic. He is chairman of several U.S. government commissions and boards.